Dressmaking for Real Women

Dressmaking
for Real Women

Lorna Knight

BARRON'S

A QUARTO BOOK

First edition for the United States, its territories and
dependencies, and Canada published in 2012 by
Barron's Educational Series, Inc.

All inquiries should be addressed to:
Barron's Educational Series, Inc.
250 Wireless Boulevard
Hauppauge, NY 11788
www.barronseduc.com

ISBN-13: 978-1-4380-0095-4

Library of Congress Control Number: 2012938760

QUAR.UDPS

Conceived, designed, and produced by:
Quarto Publishing plc
The Old Brewery
6 Blundell Street
London N7 9BH

Project editor: Chelsea Edwards
Art editor and designer: Jackie Palmer
Art director: Caroline Guest
Photographer: Martin Norris
Illustrators: Kuo Kang Chen and Tracy Turnbull
Picture researcher: Sarah Bell
Copyeditor: Ruth Patrick
Proofreader: Liz Jones
Indexer: Helen Snaith

Creative director: Moira Clinch
Publisher: Paul Carslake

Color separation by Modern Age Repro House Ltd, Hong Kong
Printed by Hung Hing Off-set Printing Co. Ltd, China
10 9 8 7 6 5 4 3 2 1

Contents

Introduction

As is the case for many people, it was my mother who introduced me to sewing when I was about six or seven years old. She continued to encourage me to make my own clothes throughout my teens until I was hooked and left home to study the subject at college.

With a life-long passion for sewing and garment making this book has given me the opportunity to share my experience in creating well-fitting clothes for all figure shapes and sizes. As well as advising on fashion choices you will find out how to adapt patterns and adjust prototype garments to fit perfectly.

Also included are notes on selecting fabrics, gathering together the most relevant tools and equipment, and the core techniques required to achieve a great finish. The information in this book provides a comprehensive reference for making clothes for real women.

Lorna Knight

About this book

One size does not fit all and this is why having the skills to adapt a commercial pattern will ensure that you get the best fit for your body shape. This book guides you through the process of selecting, understanding, and altering patterns so that you can create an outstanding, well-fitting garment.

Tools and materials

This section lists the key pieces of equipment you will use for dressmaking and adjusting patterns. The fabric directory covers a variety of materials and provides comprehensive information on qualities and uses.

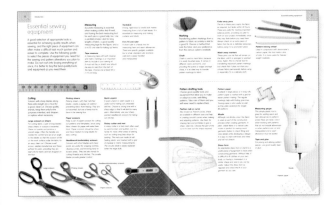

Preparation: Knowing your shape

This chapter will help you to assess your own figure type through accurate measuring, and will highlight fabrics and garments that should be sought out or avoided.

Illustration demonstrates the type of clothing that works well for that figure shape.

Diagram shows body landmarks to measure.

Recommended fabrics are listed in these panels.

Diagrams show good and bad clothing styles for each figure shape.

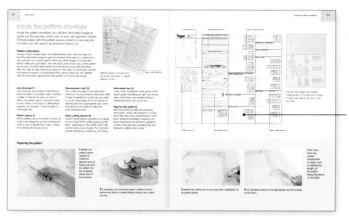

Preparation: Understanding patterns

This chapter will help you to decipher the pattern envelope information and will also cover getting the most from your fabric when laying it out.

Annotated pattern key.

Adapting patterns

This chapter looks at a whole host of areas where you may want to adjust a pattern.

Illustrations showcase well-fitting garments.

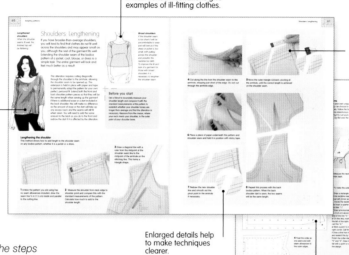

These boxed illustrations give examples of ill-fitting clothes.

Step-by-step photographs guide you through each technique.

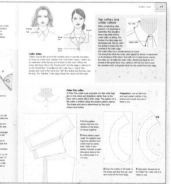

Enlarged details help to make techniques clearer.

Examples of how to draw some pattern pieces for style variations.

Making a toile

This chapter takes you through the steps for making a toile. This will allow you to iron out any problems before constructing the finished garment.

Assembly of the toile is shown on a dress form.

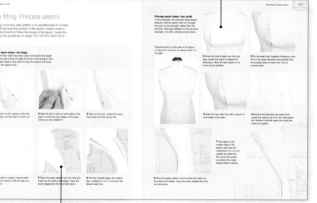

Step-by-step images show you how to use your toile to adjust the pattern.

Core techniques

Covering everything from seams and hems to fastenings and linings, this refresher section will act as a guide for beginners and a reminder for those already experienced in dressmaking.

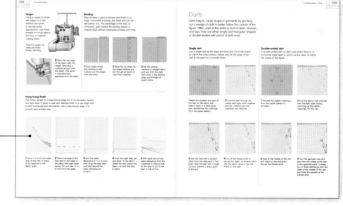

Simple diagrams show you how to complete each technique.

Essential sewing equipment

A good selection of appropriate tools is essential for achieving quality results when sewing, and the right piece of equipment can often make a difficult task much quicker and easier to complete. Use the following guide to select the pieces of equipment you need for the sewing and pattern alterations you plan to make. Do not rush into buying everything at once; it is better to buy the best-quality tools and equipment as you need them.

Measuring

Accurate measuring is essential when making clothes that fit well, and having the best measuring tool for each job is a great help, too. Use a yardstick (meter ruler) for long lengths of fabric, a good-quality measuring tape for the figure, and a 6 in (15 cm) ruler for taking up hems.

Tape measure

A measuring tape with both imperial and metric markings is an important item to include in your sewing kit. It must not fray or stretch and should be easy to read from the start of the tape. Choose one at least 60 in (115 cm) long.

Yardstick

A long, rigid wood or metal stick makes measuring from a roll or bale easier. It is essential for measuring and can be useful for large garment pieces.

6 in (15 cm) ruler

A short ruler is a handy tool for measuring hem and seam allowances. There are specific gadgets available, but a small, standard ruler functions well and is easily handled and manipulated.

Cutting

Scissors with sharp blades along their entire length are a must for a good, clean cut. Choose quality brands, keep them only for the purposes intended, and sharpen or replace when necessary.

Large scissors or shears

For cutting fabric, a pair of long-bladed, sharp shears or scissors is essential. These cut quickly and produce a smooth edge. Often the handles are molded for comfort and are at an angle to the blades so that the scissors sit flat on the work surface under the fabric for an easy, clean cut. Choose a well-known, reliable manufacturer and these will last for years, providing they are kept only for fabric and not dropped on the floor.

Pinking shears

Pinking shears, with their notched blades, create a zigzag cut useful in preventing fabric from fraying. They are not essential, but are a handy tool to have in the sewing box.

Paper scissors

Keep a pair of paper scissors for cutting out patterns and templates, since using fabric shears for paper will make them blunt. Paper scissors should be sharp and have medium to long blades for easy cutting.

Needlework/embroidery scissors

Scissors with short blades and sharp points are useful for snipping notches, clipping curves, and trimming hard-to-access areas. They are also handy for cutting threads and stitches. The smaller blades provide greater control.

Quick-unpick

A quick-unpick or seam ripper is a useful tool for taking out unwanted stitches. Choose a strong one with a sharp edge so that it will last for many years. Alternatively, use your sharp-pointed needlework scissors for taking out stitches.

Rotary cutter and mat

A rotary cutter is a tool most often used by patchworkers and quilters, but it is handy for many other areas of sewing, such as cutting long bias strips for binding. The mats are made of self-healing plastic and marked with a grid of imperial or metric measurements. The circular blade is easily replaced when the edge dulls.

Needlework/embroidery scissors

Large scissors

Pinking shears

Paper scissors

Marking

Transferring pattern markings from a pattern to fabric accurately is vital for a good fit. Choose a method that suits the fabric and your preference from the various options available.

Chalk

Chalk is used to mark fabric because it is easily brushed away. It comes in different colors and forms, and providing the points or edges are kept sharp, it is an ideal way to transfer pattern markings to fabric.

Fade-away pens

The ink in these pens marks the fabric as required, but fades within 48 hours. These are useful for marking important balance points, providing you plan to work on your project immediately, since they may fade before you need them. Always check on an extra piece of fabric that the ink is definitely temporary before using it in a prominent place.

Wash-away markers

These pens use ink that will remain on the fabric until it is sponged or washed away. Again, this is a handy tool for transferring important pattern markings, but check that it does not stain your chosen fabric permanently before using it, especially if it is a delicate cloth.

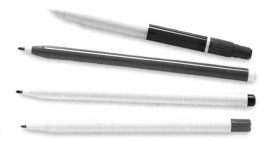

Pattern-tracing wheel

Used in conjunction with dressmaker's carbon paper, this tool marks a line of dots. It is more useful for heavier-weight materials.

Pattern drafting tools

Choose good-quality tools and equipment that allow you to make or adapt accurate, well-fitting patterns. Take care of them and you will never need to replace them.

Fashion rule or curve

Also known as French curves, these are available in different sizes and help in creating smooth curves when making and adapting patterns. Use them for shaping hips and armholes to give a sharp, clear line. Choose the part of the curve to best suit the shape required.

Pattern paper

Available in large pieces or in long rolls, pattern paper is marked with a grid for easier pattern making. The regular markings help with finding grain lines. Tracing paper is also useful as well as fine, plain cardstock for longer-life patterns.

Muslin

Although not strictly a tool, this fabric is used as part of the construction process when creating garments. A plain, stable fabric in a natural color, muslin is perfect for making mock garments (toiles) to check fitting and style details while developing a design. It is easy to mark with lines and notes and will not stretch.

Dress form

An adjustable dress form or stand is a useful piece of equipment to have when constructing garments. Without help, it is difficult to fit clothes on your own body, so having a mannequin in a similar shape and size to you can be useful. Adjust the dress form as required and check the fit of your garment as you sew.

Measuring gauge

This simple plastic tool is great for adding seam and hem allowances to patterns where there are none. Use it when working with patterns that do not include allowances or when patterns are cut and manipulated and a seam allowance must be added.

Tape and glue

For joining and altering pattern pieces, use good-quality tape or glue.

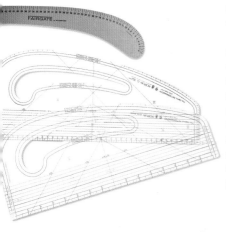

Muslin

Pattern paper

Pins and needles

Pins and needles are necessary to hold pieces of fabric and paper together when making clothes on a temporary or permanent basis. Replace them when they become bent or tarnished to avoid damaging the fabric.

Hand-sewing needles

There is a needle for every hand-sewing task, whether it is basting, hemming, darning, or embroidery. Choose appropriately, remembering that a small needle encourages smaller, neater stitches. If threading causes a problem, there are gadgets to help, or buy self-threading needles with a slot in the top of the eye.

Sewing-machine needles

It is important to use the right type of machine needle for each project. This will depend on the fabric and task. Needles have been developed to easily cope with the ever-changing fabrics available to us, including synthetic and stretch varieties. The size of the hole, the diameter of the shaft, the length of the groove, and the point all vary, and there is a type suitable for every occasion.

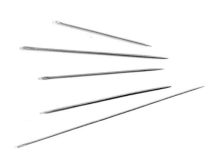

Pins

Use pins for holding paper patterns in place when cutting fabric and to hold fabric panels together while seaming. Choose long, fine pins to work with. These will cause less damage to fabric. Pins with large pearl heads are useful as they are easy to see in thicker, loosely woven fabric and you can find them quickly if they fall on the floor.

Machines

A reliable sewing machine is the most important machine to own if you want to make up-to-date clothes, although there are other machines to consider as well. An iron is essential, and a serger will produce quick and neat seams with a professional finish. Take time to choose the machines that suit you.

Sewing machine

A sewing machine is essential for anything but small projects and embroidery. It allows strong seams to be created and finished neatly, as well as producing many other more decorative techniques. Choosing the right sewing machine is likely to be one of the most important decisions for anyone who sews, so take your time and research thoroughly. If making clothes is your main interest, a good basic range of stitches (at least a good straight stitch, zigzag, and buttonhole) is needed as well as a variety of interchangeable presser feet for carrying out different techniques.

Serger

Sergers sew and finish seams in one process, speeding up garment-making and giving a more manufactured finish. They are not essential for home sewing, but having owned one, you would likely never be without one again. Sergers are generally available in three- and four-thread versions. Some models may take up to eight cones of thread and these carry out other functions as well as basic serging.

Irons

An iron plays a vital part in garment making, helping to improve the finish and making the steps of construction easier to handle. A steam iron that also operates as a dry iron is a practical option. Choose one with good steam pressure for more of an impact on the fabric. If you prefer not to have a combined model, buy a dry iron and invest in a steam-generating one as well. These irons have a separate water tank and the steam pressure is much greater, giving better results. This gives a dry option for ironing paper and fabrics that can potentially be marked by water and the high-pressure steam useful for tailoring.

Presser feet

Sewing machines have a range of alternative feet that can be attached when you are sewing different tasks. See what is available for your make and model of machine to make sewing easier.

Standard foot

The standard foot is generally the one on your machine when you buy it, and it is ideal for most basic sewing tasks. It has a smooth underside that glides over the fabric while the stitches are being formed.

Zipper foot

Use this when inserting a zipper in a conventional lapped or centered method. It allows the needle to get closer to the teeth of the zipper for a strong, neat finish. This foot is also useful for sewing piping.

Invisible/concealed zipper foot

This specialist foot tips the teeth of the zipper to the side, enabling the needle to stitch very close to the teeth to give a virtually invisible finish. The appearance of a concealed zipper foot varies between makes and models.

Walking foot

The underside of a walking foot has plastic teeth, and these, in addition to its lifting and lowering action, help to feed layers of fabric evenly past the needle so that regular stitches are formed. Use it when sewing thick cloth, several layers, or stretchy fabric.

Rolled hem foot

When a delicate hem is required in a soft or fine fabric, use a rolled hem foot to twist and sew a very narrow hem. A rolled hem can be sewn by hand or produced with a serger, but this presser foot makes it possible to create a good rolled hem finish with a sewing machine.

Overcast foot

If a serger is not available for finishing edges, use an overcast foot. Set the machine for zigzag or an overcasting stitch. Lower the foot so that the metal finger sits right on the cut edge, then sew. The threads form the stitches over the fabric edge without pulling on it and give a neat finish.

Threads

Threads for all sewing situations are abundant, whether for hand stitching or for use with a machine or serger. Make use of the many varieties to get the best results every time.

All-purpose thread

Spun from cotton or polyester, general-purpose threads are ideal for use with the sewing machine. Choose thread from a well-known manufacturer and in a color close to that of the fabric being used.

Basting thread

Thread specifically for hand basting is made from soft cotton. It is weaker than standard thread and breaks more easily so it is unlikely to damage the fabric when temporary basting stitches are removed.

Topstitch thread

This strong and thick thread gives a bolder finish when stitched onto fabric. Use it with a topstitch needle as this has a thicker shaft and a larger eye. Increase the stitch length to 8 spi (3 mm).

Silk thread

Use silk thread for very special projects in silk or woolen fabric and for hand sewing hems, because it tends to knot and tangle less. Polyester is a cheaper alternative.

Serger thread

Serger thread comes on large reels or cones because sergers use a great deal of thread when stitching and finishing edges.

Machine-embroidery floss

For decorative, embroidered designs and to embellish garments, use machine-embroidery floss. It is generally made from rayon or polyester with a high sheen, although embroidery threads are also available in cotton and wool, which give a matte finish.

Bobbin fill

Bobbin fill is a very fine white or black thread used in the bobbin when sewing with embroidery threads. It is useful because it is less expensive than embroidery floss and because it is fine, a much longer length can be wound onto the bobbin for less-frequent refilling.

Hand-embroidery floss

Embroidery floss for hand use includes pearle cotton and stranded silk. While these threads are too thick to pass through a machine needle, they can be used for couching where machine zigzag stitches cover and attach these thicker threads to the surface of fabric. These thicker threads can also be wound onto the bobbin of a sewing machine and with the fabric reversed (upside down), stitched directly to fabric.

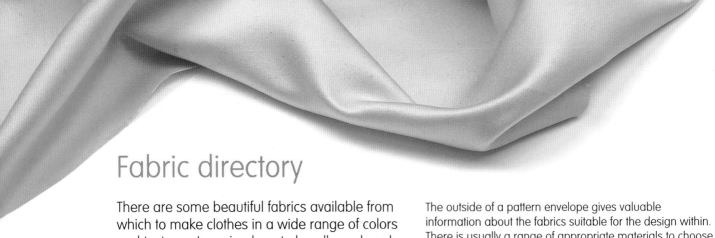

Fabric directory

There are some beautiful fabrics available from which to make clothes in a wide range of colors and textures. Learning how to handle and work with different fabrics can take years, so use the guide on the following pages to help develop your knowledge so you can choose wisely.

The outside of a pattern envelope gives valuable information about the fabrics suitable for the design within. There is usually a range of appropriate materials to choose from, allowing everyone the opportunity to find something to suit their own individual taste. In addition, it will also advise on the amount of material you need to buy, depending on the width of the roll. Make use of this information to avoid buying too much or too little fabric.

FIBER AND FABRIC FACTS

There are two important pieces of information you need to know when choosing fabric: The fiber that it is made from and the way the material is constructed. With this knowledge you will be able to make appropriate decisions about how to get the best results.

Fibers

Natural fibers are individual filaments found in plants and animal hair that are gathered together and used to form yarns and fabrics. The most common plant fibers used for fabric are cotton (from the boll of the cotton plant) and linen (from the stem of the flax plant) although hemp, jute, and ramie are also used to create coarse textiles. Animal fibers include wool (from sheep, goats, and llamas for example) and silk (from the cocoon of the silk moth).

Natural fibers have been used for cloth making for centuries, but in more recent years, man-made and synthetic resources have been produced to broaden the range of fabrics available. These have been developed in search of particular characteristics such as their handling and laundering properties, or to recreate expensive natural fabrics more cheaply.

The original man-made fibers, described as artificial, were viscose or rayon, which come from regenerated cellulose using wood pulp or short cotton fibers and acetate that is derived from acetic acid.

The true synthetic fibers—nylon, polyester, and acrylic—are petroleum-based and were invented during the middle of the twentieth century.

The most recent addition to the garment fiber industry is Spandex, and with its incredible stretch and recovery properties, it is often used with other fibers to produce stretchy fabric.

Blending fabrics is very common and allows different fiber features to be combined; for example, polyester and cotton is a quick-drying and absorbent fabric often used for shirts or bed linen; when knitted, cotton and Spandex produce a stretchy, absorbent fabric that is ideal for sportswear.

Fabric

The yarn or thread formed by spinning the fiber filaments is woven or knitted to produce cloth ready for garment making. The only exception to this is where the fibers are matted together to form a bonded fabric, or felt. This method is often used for crafts, disposable overalls, or interfacings and less often for fashion clothing due to its lack of strength.

Fashion fabric is generally dyed and the surface is often printed. Alternatively, the detail in the fabric may be created by weaving or knitting different-colored threads to form a pattern.

Fabric may be finished with a treatment to improve its handle or properties; for example, linen and cotton may be made crease-proof and wool made moth-proof or shrink-proof.

The way the fabric has been constructed and the original fiber content both affect its handling. Find out as much information as possible about the cloth you choose for a specific project and experiment with small pieces before starting to cut and sew. This gives you the best opportunity to produce a perfect design creation.

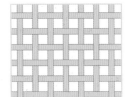

Interwoven yarns create a stable fabric.

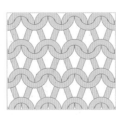

Knitted loops give a flexible, stretchy cloth.

Matted fibers form a felted material that is seldom used for fashion clothing.

Woven fabrics

Generally, medium-weight, woven fabrics are easy to handle and are the best choice for beginners. Stiff and bulky fabrics or those that are fine with little body are more difficult to sew with.

Denim

Structure: Plain, woven cotton.
Description: Originally designed for workwear, this blue cotton fabric is absorbent, strong, and hardwearing. Available in medium and heavy weight, and popular as a fashion fabric for casual wear.
Uses: Choose lightweight denim for shirts or dresses and heavier examples for jeans, skirts, and casual jackets.
Tips: Use a strong jeans needle and lengthen the sewing machine stitch to 8 spi (3 mm). Plain and flat-fell seams work well and topstitching in a contrasting thread is a popular finish.

Cotton lawn

Structure: Cotton, plain weave.
Description: A smooth, fine, and lightweight fabric sometimes plain and often printed.
Uses: Ideal for dresses, shirts, blouses, and lingerie. Can be used on the inside as an underlining to add body or depth to a fashion fabric.
Tips: Use long-bladed sharp shears for a clean-cut edge and sew with a standard size 9 sewing-machine needle and a stitch length of 12–10 spi (2–2.5 mm). Plain and French seams work well and decorative stitching, with twin or wing needles, creates an attractive decorative finish.

Muslin

Structure: Closely woven cotton.
Description: This plain-finished, stable, unbleached cotton fabric is available in various weights.
Uses: Use this for test garments, or toiles, when developing a design to check the fit and style. Muslin is also popular for craft projects and bag making.

Tips: Use a standard needle in a size to suit the weight of the cloth and choose a 10 spi (2.5 mm) stitch length. Use plain seams to join fabric pieces.

Linen

Structure: Plain-weave natural cloth.
Description: Linen has an obvious plain weave and a tendency to wrinkle unless treated.
Uses: It is a classic choice for jackets, pants, skirts, and suits, while lighter weights make good shirts and dresses.
Tips: Cut with sharp scissors to give a good clean edge. Work quickly, since linen has a tendency to unravel. Consider neatening raw edges before construction. Sew with a standard needle and use a medium stitch length of 10 spi (2.5 mm). Choose plain and flat-fell seams.

Chiffon

Structure: Plain weave in silk or synthetic fiber.
Description: This transparent cloth is soft and sheer. It was traditionally made from silk but polyester is commonly used today.
Uses: Popular for skirts, blouses, and scarves and often used in multiple layers or with a lining below.
Tips: Cut chiffon with long-bladed, sharp scissors and sew with a new size 9 standard sewing-machine needle to avoid snags. Shorten the stitch to 12 spi (2 mm) and use French seams for a tidy finish.

Shirting

Structure: Woven cotton, silk, linen, or polyester-and-cotton mix.
Description: A fine-weight cloth, generally with a smooth finish, either plain, printed, or with a woven stripe or check.
Uses: Shirts, blouses, and dresses.
Tips: Use a standard needle in a fine or medium size (9–11), depending on the weight of the cloth, with a medium stitch length of 10 spi (2.5 mm). Choose plain, flat-fell, and French seams for construction.

Silks

This natural fiber is made by unraveling and spinning the cocoon of the silkworm into silk threads, which are then woven into fabric.

Silk dupion

Structure: Plain-weave silk.
Description: This is a crisp fabric with an uneven texture because of the slubs in the threads it is woven from. It has a dull sheen.
Uses: Jackets, suits, dresses, and pants, generally for evening or occasion wear.
Tips: As it unravels badly, consider neatening the raw edges before construction. Use a standard size 11 sewing-machine needle to sew with and choose silk or polyester thread. Use plain seams to join panels.

Silk organza

Structure: Plain-weave silk.
Description: This transparent fabric is woven from highly spun threads, making it fine, strong, and crisp.
Uses: Use it for evening wear backed with lining. 100 percent silk organza is a useful underlining providing support without adding depth or weight to a fashion fabric.
Tips: Sew with a fine size 9 sewing-machine needle and use French or hairline seams for a delicate join. Sew with silk or polyester thread.

Silk satin

Structure: Silk woven into satin (polyester and acetate fibers are also popular).
Description: A satin fabric reflects light because of the many flat threads that lie on the surface, so it has a shiny finish.
Uses: The surface threads are easily damaged, so this makes it a delicate fabric more suited to special occasion and evening wear.
Tips: Use a new, sharp, Microtex needle to prevent damaging the threads in the weave and sew with a 10 spi (2.5 mm) stitch length. Plain and French seams work well. Sew with silk or polyester thread.

nim

Muslin

Linen

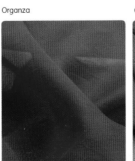
Organza

Chiffon

Satin

Habotai

Structure: Plain-weave silk (polyester fiber may also be used).

Description: This fine and plain fabric is very soft and lightweight.

Uses: Use habotai silk for lingerie items and blouses. It is also ideal as a lining fabric for coats, jackets, and skirts.

Tips: Cut with long, sharp blades or use a rotary cutter with a self-healing mat (see page 8). Choose a fine (size 9) Microtex needle and small stitch length, 12 spi (2 mm), for seaming. French seams are a good choice. Change the needle frequently to avoid damage to the silk. Use silk or polyester thread.

Wools and wool mixes

Wool fabrics vary enormously, depending on the breed from which the fibers come, whether they are used alone or mixed with other fibers, and how the fabric is constructed. Woolen fabric can be used for making pants, coats, or chunky knitted sweaters.

Worsted wool

Structure: Plain- or twill-weave wool.

Description: A worsted-wool yarn is produced from long, combed fibers that are highly twisted. It is smooth, strong, and fine.

Uses: Use worsted wool for suits, jackets, skirts, and pants.

Tips: Cut with sharp shears and sew with a standard size 11 needle with good-quality polyester thread. Use a medium stitch length of 10 spi (2.5 mm) and join panels with plain seams pressed open. Take care when pressing and use a pressing cloth to protect the surface and prevent a shine from appearing.

Wool crepe

Structure: Twisted weave.

Description: Crepe fabric can be made from wool but also silk, synthetic fibers, or a mix. Crepe has a pebbly surface and tends not to wrinkle. Although woven, the fabric may have a slight stretch to it.

Uses: Crepe is suitable for dresses, pants, and skirts and works best for soft, draping styles.

Tips: Preshrink crepe before cutting out and sew with a standard size 11 needle with a 10 spi (2.5 mm) stitch length. Construct garments with plain seams pressed open or use a serger.

Bouclé

Structure: Woven or knitted with a textured yarn.

Description: Generally made from wool or a wool-and-synthetic mix of fibers, bouclé has a thick surface textured with curly, twisted loops.

Uses: Bouclé fabric is popular for coats, jackets, and cardigans.

Tips: Cut fabric pieces with sharp shears and sew with a stretch needle in a size 12. Choose a longer stitch length of 10–8 spi (2.5–3 mm) and opt for a stretch stitch or narrow zigzag if the fabric is very stretchy.

Loose-weave tweed

Structure: Loosely woven yarns of wool, silk, or synthetic fibers, or a blend.

Description: Loosely woven tweed is generally made from thicker yarns for a luxurious look. Although woven, it may not be stable, and the yarns unravel easily from its cut edges.

Uses: Use any tweed fabric for jackets and coats.

Tips: Consider neatening the edges immediately after cutting and before sewing. Alternatively, cut a lightweight, fusible interfacing and back all pieces to reduce fraying and stabilize panels. Use a size 11 or 12 needle and a 10–8 spi (2.5–3 mm) stitch length. Finish garments with a lining or bind raw edges.

Tartan and checks

Structure: Twill-weave wool or wool-mix fibers.

Description: The pattern within the fabric is created by different-colored yarns woven in a sequence through the cloth. The weave may be tight or loose.

Uses: Tartan is more popular during some seasons than others and is used for kilts, skirts, pants, jackets, and coats.

Tips: Take care when placing pattern pieces on fabric to account for matching at the seams. Sew with a standard size 11 or 12 needle and use a 10–8 spi (2.5–3 mm) stitch length. Fit a walking foot to the sewing machine to help feed the fabric evenly and make matching seams easier.

Wool coating

Structure: Woven wool or mixed fibers.

Description: A coating is a thick and warm cloth.

Uses: As implied by the name, this fabric is used for coats and winter jackets.

Tips: The problems when sewing this cloth occur because of its thickness. When seaming, the upper layer tends to slide over the lower layer, so fit a walking foot to help encourage an even feed. Cut with long-bladed scissors and sew with a large size 14 machine needle. Extend the stitch length to 8 spi (3 mm) because this will work better with the thick fabric.

Knitted fabric

Knit fabrics are constructed with loops rather than warp and weft threads being woven together. The fibers used to make the threads/yarns for knit fabric may be natural wool, cotton, or synthetic, or various blends of these, creating a multitude of knit fabrics.

Cotton knit

Structure: Knit

Description: Light- to medium-weight stretchy cotton. It is very absorbent and stretches as the fabric is pulled. When mixed with Spandex, the stretch-and-recovery properties are even better. The fabric may be dyed a solid color or, as an alternative, it can be surface-printed.

Uses: Most commonly used for T-shirts, but also for dresses, skirts, and underwear.

Tips: Use a stretch needle and choose a stretch stitch if one is available on the sewing

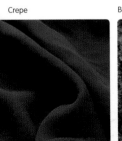
Crepe

Bouclé

Cotton tweed

Donegal tweed

Tartan

Cotton knit

machine. If not, set a zigzag to a standard length and narrow width so the seam line will move if the fabric is pulled. A serger is a good tool to use for cotton knit fabric.

Slinky knit
Structure: Knitted viscose/rayon.
Description: Viscose/rayon is a heavy yarn that has a slinky handle, and when knitted, it stretches and drapes beautifully.
Uses: As it is available in different weights, use this for dresses, skirts, cardigans, and unstructured jackets intended to drape.
Tips: Place the fabric on a work surface covered with a cotton sheet to prevent it from moving or slipping when cutting. Fit a stretch needle and set to stretch stitch when using a sewing machine. A walking foot helps to feed the fabric more evenly, too. Sew with a serger if one is available.

Sweatshirt fabric
Structure: Knit.
Description: Although more stable than many other knitted fabrics, cotton sweatshirting does stretch and pull. It has a knitted surface with a soft backing.
Uses: Sports clothing and leisure wear. This is a comfortable and warm cloth. Use sweatshirt fabric for loose-fitting pants, sweatshirts, and casual zippered jackets.
Tips: Choose a stretch or ball-point needle in a size 12 or 14 and sew with a serger or, if using a sewing machine, a stretch stitch and walking foot. Hem with a twin needle to imitate a manufactured stitch.

Bonded fabrics
Some specially created materials are designed for the internal construction of clothing and are not visible on the outside. These interfacings are essential for producing a perfect finish.

Interfacing
Structure: Matted fibers.
Description: A material produced from bonded fibers, not intended to be seen, and used for an internal layer to support collars, cuffs, and facings. It does not fray or stretch.
Uses: Use to stiffen collars, cuffs, and facings.
Tips: Choose a suitable weight for the fabric being used and opt for a lighter-weight interfacing if in doubt, as a "too-crisp" finish can sometimes result. Trim away from seam allowances to reduce bulk.

Special-occasion fabrics
Occasion wear makes use of the most luxurious and expensive fabrics. Fibers from all sources are constructed in a variety of ways to create special fabrics and garments.

Velvet
Structure: Woven (sometimes knitted) backing with dense pile on surface.
Description: Made from silk, cotton, viscose/rayon, or polyester fibers, velvet varies and this affects its handling. It is a thick material with a luxurious pile held in place by its backing. Velvets on a knitted base drape well.
Uses: Suitable for jackets, skirts, bodices, and special-occasion wear. Velvets that drape well are ideal for skirts and dresses.
Tips: Cut all pieces in the same direction to avoid differences in the way the light catches the panels. Iron with care, using a piece of the same velvet and very delicate pressure to avoid crushing the pile. Use a size 12 standard needle and a 8 spi (3 mm) stitch length. Use plain seams and finger press. If fitting a zipper, insert a concealed version so there will be no topstitching.

Lace
Structure: Sewn on net, or a knitted or crochet construction. It may be stable or stretchy.
Description: Lace is a delicate transparent fabric with an intricate pattern or design incorporated. It varies a great deal in quality and price and is available as all-over lace on the roll or as edging in various widths.
Uses: Use edging lace for trimming skirts, dresses, blouses, and lingerie. All-over lace is perfect for wedding dresses and nightgowns.
Tips: Pin with long, large-headed pins and sew with a fine size 9 machine needle. Lap the seams to retain the design in the pattern and sew with a zigzag, then cut away the excess.

Imitation fabrics
The advent of these fabrics has allowed the look of animal fur and skin to be used without having to harm any animals in the process.

Faux fur
Structure: A knitted base with a dense pile.
Description: Faux fur imitates animal fur of all types and is dyed accordingly. The length of the dense pile and quality of the finish varies.
Uses: Generally faux fur in fashion is used for coats, waistcoats, hats, and trims.
Tips: Cut through the backing fabric with needlework or embroidery scissors, then tease the pile fibers apart to avoid spreading the fur all over the room. Sew with a stretch needle and use a short, narrow zigzag stitch to sew the backing together when joining panels.

Faux suede
Structure: Knit.
Description: Most modern examples look very realistic, but are much easier to launder and keep clean than real suede.
Uses: Use faux suede for coats, jackets, pants, and bags.
Tips: Place all pattern pieces in the same direction for cutting. Use a Microtex needle to sew with a 10 spi (2.5 mm) straight stitch. Sew with a good-quality polyester thread. Flat-fell seams make a good finish.

olyester and Lycra

Underlining

Velvet

Stretch raschel lace

Lace

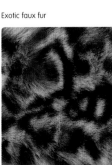
Exotic faux fur

Preparation:
Knowing your shape, understanding patterns

An advantage of making your own clothes is that you can tailor them to your unique measurements; however, it's also important to buy patterns for clothing styles that will work for you. This section explains where to get patterns from and includes hints on size selection and how to decipher the information and symbols.

Measuring

For clothes to fit our three-dimensional bodies we need to have a good idea of our general shape, along with detailed figure dimensions. With accurate measurements, personal patterns can be created to fit an individual perfectly. This type of styling is expensive and most home sewers, who do not have an in-depth knowledge of pattern cutting, must rely on commercial patterns produced from standard measurements. This allows us all to create pieces of clothing that almost meet our body shape requirements. After some tweaking, we can achieve a great fit.

Choose a measuring tape that gives both metric and imperial measurements for more versatile use, such as the one shown here. An extra long one is particularly useful too.

General measuring rules

When using a standard pattern, you must have accurate body measurements so that you can choose the size closest to your own silhouette. Follow the rules below for easy and precise measuring:

- Get a friend to help you take your measurements. It is hard to reach certain areas and to make sure the tape measure is level where you cannot see it. This also makes the process more enjoyable and less of a chore.

- Use a full-length mirror to check that you are placing the tape measure in the correct places and between the right points. Even if you have a friend to help, a mirror is helpful for you both.

- Wear well-fitting undergarments when taking measurements and do not take your measurements over clothing. You need to have complete access to every limb and body part to find out its length and circumference.

- Stand tall, with your feet together, and do not breathe in. You need to have truthful figures to work from.

- Measure accurately, making sure the tape is flat and starts and finishes at the proper points. Use the fitting guide opposite to help you to know how to take each measurement.

- Place the tape firmly (but not too tight) around the body and do not leave any slack. Ease is built into the pattern for comfort and style, so there is no need to add any more.

Body landmarks

Horizontal:

1 Bust: Hold the tape level and measure the fullest part of the bust. A well-fitting bra is essential in achieving this.

2 Waist: Tie a length of soft elastic lightly around your middle and it will automatically fall into the waist position. Measure at this point.

3 Hip: This is the fullest part of the bottom, and its position varies from one person to another.

4 Chest: Measure across the center front, just above the bust, from armhole to armhole approximately 3 in (7.5 cm) below the neck level.

5 Back width: Measure across the center back between the armholes, approximately 6 in (15 cm) below the prominent neck bone.

6 Shoulder: Take this measurement from the neck edge to the shoulder bone.

7 Upper arm: Place the tape measure around the bicep, while the arm is slightly bent, with your hand on your waist or hip.

8 Wrist: Measure the wrist with a small amount of ease.

Vertical:

9 Height: Mark your height against a wall, without shoes and with your feet together, with your heels to the wall.

10 Nape to waist: Measure from the prominent bone in your neck to the waist using the elastic method to highlight your waist position.

11 Shoulder to front waist: Measure from the shoulder, over the bust point, to the waist.

12 Arm length: With your hand on your hip, measure from the shoulder bone to the wrist, following the bend of the elbow.

13 Waist to hip: Measure from waist level to the hip. This is often a standard measurement but knowing how you compare to the standard is important for making appropriate alterations.

14 Waist to floor: Measure from waist level to the floor, following the contour of the hip.

15 Waist to knee: Measure from waist level to mid-knee.

16 Crotch depth: Sit on a chair and measure from the waist to the seat level. See page 120.

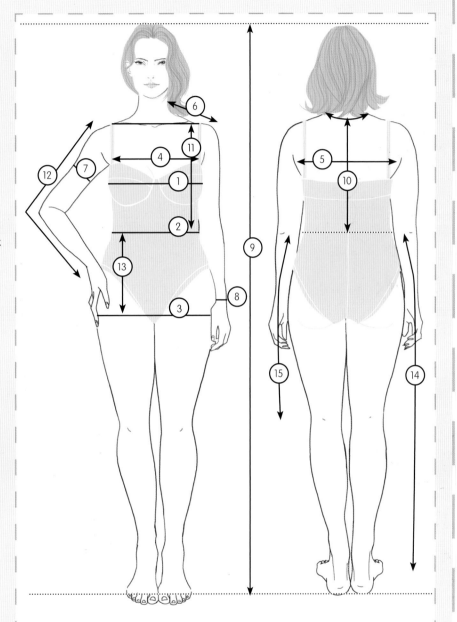

Hourglass

This very feminine figure type is probably the outline that is most desired by women. It is a well-proportioned and balanced shape, which gives the opportunity to select clothes to highlight the curves rather than hide them. Throughout history, rigid corsets and underskirt structures, such as the farthingale or bustle, were worn to emphasize a shapely silhouette, creating a narrow waist and fullness around the hip, bottom, and bust. Even today—with a little help from materials such as Lycra and Spandex—many women aspire to a narrow waist and flat stomach balanced with a larger bust and hip.

The owner of an hourglass figure should choose soft, fluid styles that drape over the body in knitted, bias-cut, and flowing fabrics. Tailored styles and crisp fabrics tend to create an oversized look on a curvy hourglass, so select romantic, draping fabrics in solid colors and pretty prints to flow over the body.

It is important to maintain balance when dressing an hourglass shape, providing the same emphasis to both bust and hip and avoiding the addition of too much fullness to one or the other. Follow the line of the figure with close-fitting, but not constricting, clothing to show off the outline.

Selecting the most flattering style
Choose simple, fitted jackets without the fuss or detail of bold pockets or large, prominent buttons. Blouses, tops, and T-shirts made from knitted cotton or rayon, which follow the outline of the body, emphasize a small waist. Wrap styles work particularly well too.

Bias-cut and slinky knit skirts, with a fitted band rather than elastic at the waist, are great for the curvy hourglass. If a full style is chosen for a skirt, balance this by adding width across the bust and shoulders. Choose a bold collar design, stronger pattern, or colored fabric for the upper half of the body.

Go for dresses that accentuate the shape with princess seaming, an asymmetric wrap, or a bias-cut shift style. Shorter women should raise the position of the waist to add leg length. For evening wear, consider a boned bodice to highlight the figure shape.

Styles to avoid
Pants in a simple line with a smooth waist and hip, without emphasis on pockets and fastenings, look good. All leg styles are suitable for an hourglass shape, but avoid those that are very narrow at the ankle.

This well-fitting dress emphasizes the shapely curves of the hourglass figure.

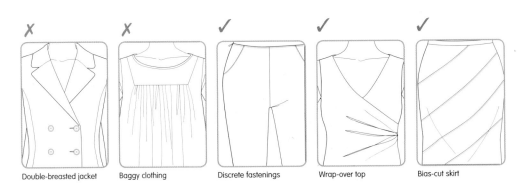

Double-breasted jacket   Baggy clothing   Discrete fastenings   Wrap-over top   Bias-cut skirt

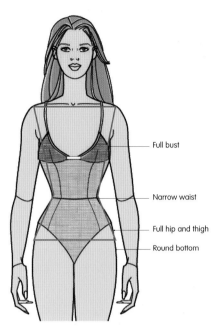

- Full bust
- Narrow waist
- Full hip and thigh
- Round bottom

Checklist

Fabrics: Materials that drape, such as wool crepe, chiffon, silk, viscose/rayon, cotton knit with Lycra/Spandex, and fine wool knits.

Pattern: Romantic and dainty fabric designs with lots of soft curves work better than bold, sharp lines and patterns on an hourglass frame.

Style elements: Well-fitting garments that show off the figure, such as bias-cut dresses and skirts, wrap-over tops and dresses, side-fastening pants with no fussy front detailing, and close-fitting jackets and coats with a minimalist approach to fastenings.

Avoid: Angular shapes, baggy clothing, and adding emphasis to any single part of the figure. Stripes and checks can make the entire frame look bigger than it really is, and double-breasted jackets and coats create the illusion of width.

Wrap-over designs, softly draping skirts, and well-fitting dresses enhance curves and flatter an hourglass figure.

Choosing the right garment fabric

- Viscose/rayon jersey knit
- Printed cotton jersey knit
- Faux suede
- Polyester or wool crepe
- Polyester jersey knit
- Fine tailored cloth with added Lycra
- Soft swirling print
- Paisley print

These fabric swatches are ideal for hourglass figures. From top to bottom: Satin, crepe, dainty embroidery, and a swirling pattern.

Bottom-heavy triangle

The classic pear-shaped figure carries more weight at the hip and thigh with less at the shoulder and bust, giving the impression of a bottom-heavy triangle. By choosing clothes carefully to emphasize the upper half of the body, any imbalance is minimized. Using style and color to draw attention to the shoulders and away from the hip creates a more balanced figure. In addition to selecting appropriate clothing in figure-flattering colors, fit is important. Excess fabric covering fuller parts of the body adds extra width and weight, while a garment that is too tight draws attention to any bulges.

The shoulder detail draws the eye up to the narrow part of the frame and away from the broad hips and thighs.

For pear-shaped figure types, choose fabrics and styles appropriate to the upper and lower body. Below the waist, choose light- to medium-weight fabrics in solid or subtly patterned designs in styles that fit closely, but not tightly, to the figure and do not add depth with gathers or frills. Balance this with layers and textures on the upper body to add volume. Use crisp cottons, linens, or bouncy frills, and perhaps thicker wools and knits. These materials, made up in suitable styles, will help to balance the proportion of a pear-shaped figure.

Selecting the most flattering styles
Opt for tops and jackets with details such as pockets, buttons, fancy collars, frills, and embroidery to draw the eye up and away from the hip. The illusion of width across the upper half of the body (to improve the proportion) can also be created with full or decorative sleeves and bold accessories in the form of jewelry and scarves.

Wearing darker colors below the waist can take attention away from the hip and thigh, but if the waist is narrow and defined, make the most of this asset and show it off. Narrow bias-cut or vertically paneled skirts that fit closely to the hip are flattering. Some broad-hipped women avoid wearing pants and feel more comfortable in skirts, though plain pants with a flat front in a flared or bootleg style flatter many pear shapes. Leg length can be increased—if needed—by wearing heels. Dresses with a high waist help to alter proportion, adding length to the leg and taking the eye up to the bust and shoulder.

Styles to avoid
For tops and blouses, any design that takes the eye to the center of the body is narrowing the frame further, so keep away from plain, high-necked T-shirts because these tend to emphasize a flat chest. Similarly, halter-neck styles and raglan sleeves accentuate narrow shoulders and draw the eye inward. Below the waist, avoid pants with many pockets and those with tucks at the waist because these add bulk where it is not needed. Narrow pants that taper to the ankle give a rounded shape to the body, drawing attention to larger hips and thighs. Jackets and tops that finish at hip level—the widest area—emphasize the width, so choose shorter-length jackets or three-quarter and longer coats.

Although it is a good idea to wear more detail on the upper half of the body, chunky, baggy sweaters result in enlarging the entire frame. Keep the outline of the body clear.

✗

Halter-neck top

✗

Raglan sleeve

✓

Capped sleeve and embroidered neckline

✓

Open-neck shirt

✓

Bold jewelry

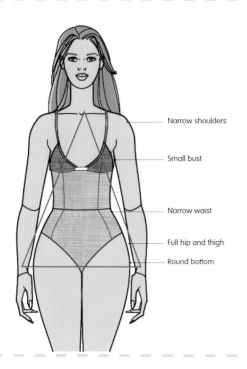

- Narrow shoulders
- Small bust
- Narrow waist
- Full hip and thigh
- Round bottom

Checklist

- **Fabrics:** Top half: Light- and medium-weight fabrics worn in layers. Textured fabrics with fancy weaves or added stitch detail like tucks, gathers, and embroidery. Crisp cotton and linen, structured knitwear.
Lower half: Solid fabrics in dark or subtle colors. Soft fabrics, cut on the bias, that drape well and skim over the hip.

- **Pattern:** Keep pattern, color, and texture for the upper half of the body and wear solid colors below the waist to visually balance the figure's proportions. Wear tops with horizontal stripes or designs that broaden the frame and use vertical stripes for skirts and pants.

- **Style elements:** Well-fitting skirts and pants in plain, fuss-free, tailored styles worn with soft, crisp tops and blouses work well. A-line and bias-cut skirts are suitable. Emphasize shoulders with small capped sleeves or sleeves gathered at the head/cap. An open-neck shirt or a rolled collar adds weight to the top of the figure, as do yoke styles with details such as tucks, embroidery, or piped seams. Short jackets and long coats are perfect for outerwear.

- **Avoid:** Large, shapeless garments, plain tops, and full and fussy skirts and pants. Fabrics with horizontal designs worn on the lower part of the body and vertical patterned fabrics on the bodice do not suit this figure shape.

Choose designs with detail at the bust and shoulder levels and plainer styles below the waist.

Choosing the right garment fabric

- Crisp cotton shirting
- Light- and medium-weight linens and linen blends
- Light- and medium-weight silk
- Cotton or polyester and cotton-blend stretch knits
- Viscose/rayon jersey knit
- Cotton poplin
- Textured knits
- Bouclé
- Fine woven wool with Spandex

These fabric swatches are ideal for the bottom-heavy triangle figure. From top to bottom: Poplin, embroidery detail, bouclé, and textured knit.

Top-heavy triangle

The inverted triangle body shape, where the shoulders are relatively broad in relation to the hips, is easily reproportioned by clever choice of clothing. In emphasizing the lower half of the body by showing off the legs and choosing elegant skirts and pants, the awareness of the bust and shoulders is minimized, and the proportion is realigned. Plain, simply styled tops with smooth-shouldered sleeves, eased in at the head or cap, help create the perception of a straighter figure silhouette. Embellishment, color, or style detail is more suited to the lower part of the figure than the bodice.

One important aspect when choosing clothes is to ensure a good fit, which may require pattern alteration to accommodate a larger bust or cup size, or adjusting the proportion so that the bust, waist, and hip are in the correct relative positions.

Selecting the most flattering styles

When choosing tops, those with round, scooped, or V-shaped necklines look good. Halter-neck garments also work well because they draw the eye to the center, taking the attention away from the shoulder width. Smooth shoulders on blouses, dresses, and jackets narrow the frame, as do long lapels that lie flat to the chest. If the lapels of a jacket are large or sit away from the body, this adds to the impression of depth and weight. Plain tops and jackets with few pockets and buttons are preferable to those with fussy details.

With narrow hips and thighs, any style of pants is suitable. Straight pencil skirts and those with pleats and panels are great for narrow-hipped figures. Waists finished with a band or facing are best, while elastic or gathered styles should be avoided. Back pockets with embroidered detail accentuate the bottom, which few other figure types can get away with.

Long coats look good whether straight, slightly nipped at the waist, or flared, with a small collar and subtle shoulders.

Styles to avoid

With this figure shape, any garment that emphasizes the shoulders should be avoided, including gathered sleeves, epaulettes, and large shoulder pads. Styles with large collars, yokes, high waist seaming, and horizontal detail across the bodice all add width to the upper body. Frills and gathers add even more depth so keep the lines smooth and straight. Double-breasted jackets and coats add unnecessary width to the frame.

The "v"-shaped neck of the wrap top draws the eye to the center in the upper half of the body, while the print of the skirt emphasizes the narrow hips and slim legs.

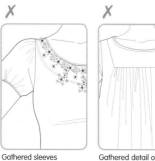
Gathered sleeves

Gathered detail on top

V-shaped neckline

Halter-neck top

Straight skirt

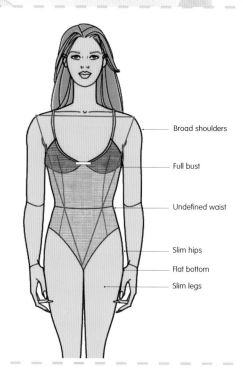

Broad shoulders

Full bust

Undefined waist

Slim hips

Flat bottom

Slim legs

Checklist

• **Fabrics:** Choose crisp, woven fabrics for a tailored look and to keep the lines smooth. Cottons, linens, and gabardine work well, as do fine wools and silks.

• **Pattern:** Keep pattern in the form of color and texture for the lower part of the body and wear solid colors above the waist to help to balance the silhouette and improve the figure proportion. Wear pants and skirts with horizontal stripes or designs that broaden the frame, and use vertical stripes for tops and blouses.

• **Style elements:** All styles of pants suit this body shape, with pockets and embellishments if you want them. Straight, pleated, and paneled skirts work well, and skirts and dresses can be worn above the knee. Keep detail to a minimum for tops and shirts, choosing plain styles with simple necklines and fuss-free sleeves. Choose structured jackets and coats with slight nipping at the waist.

• **Avoid:** Tops with fussy details, pockets, and textured finishes, big sleeves and shoulders, definition of the waist, bias-cut or full gathered skirts, and soft and draping fabrics.

Pencil skirts and skirts with fullness are flattering styles when worn with plain tops.

Choosing the right garment fabric

• Woven cotton checks and stripes
• Paisley prints
• Crisp woven cotton
• Fine wool with Spandex
• Faux suede
• Denim
• Light- and medium-weight silks and satins

These fabric swatches are ideal for the top-heavy triangle figure. From top to bottom: Gabardine, stretch gabardine, pleats, and denim.

Round

A round or apple-shaped figure carries weight in the middle of the body. The trick is to move the attention away from the central area by accentuating the face and legs and increasing height with careful choice of clothing and accessories. Fabrics and styles that drape over the body and do not cling are a good choice for this silhouette. Garments that give straight, smooth lines without adding bulk to the frame help to lengthen and narrow the shape. Use the shoulders as a frame and if necessary add shoulder pads to improve their shape, although not necessarily their width.

As always, fit is important, and loose, baggy clothing simply exaggerates rather than conceals excess weight. For this reason, long, straight, vertical lines are good, so wear longer-length, plain clothes that drape over the figure. Avoid horizontal lines across the body, especially at the wider parts like the bust and waist. Separates that meet at the waist create a line across the middle, so consider choosing a top that extends below and covers the waist of the pants or skirt. Use detail at the neckline and choose an appropriate hem length; long lengths work well, but shorter hems show off lovely legs.

Selecting the most flattering styles

Keep detail away from the broadest parts of the figure like the bust and waist. Choose long, straight jackets with a shawl collar or no collar to lead the eye vertically up and down at the center. Anything that draws attention to the waist will emphasize it, so avoid short jackets, belts, and two-piece outfits. A tunic top worn with leggings or

a straight skirt is a flattering alternative. Wear skirts with an elastic waistband for comfort but cover with a long top. Straight or wrap skirts are a good choice too with a top to cover the waistline. Narrow, straight pants with a side zipper without front tucks give a flatter finish over the stomach.

While keeping the clothing at the center of the body plain and fuss-free, use detail at the neckline or a fancy collar to draw the eye upward. Use scarves and jewelry to accessorize the neckline for the same reason.

Styles to avoid

Avoid crop tops, high-waist styles, and clothing that clings to the body. Skirts and dresses that are belted or elasticized at the waist do not flatter a rounded figure. Crisp fabrics add volume as do bright, bold colors and patterns. Details such as pockets, buttons, and embroidery should be kept away from the fuller parts of the body to avoid drawing attention to them.

The long tunic top skims the fuller part of the body, finishing at upper leg level where the body is slimmer. Detail at the neckline draws the eye upwards and away from the waist too.

✗ 	✗ 	✓ 	✓ 	✓ 
Cropped top	Belted waist	Accessories at neckline	Wrap skirt	Side-fastening pants

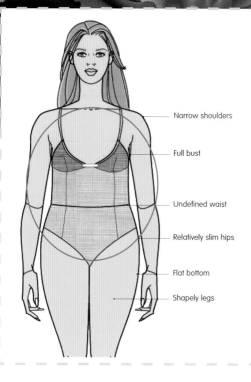

- Narrow shoulders
- Full bust
- Undefined waist
- Relatively slim hips
- Flat bottom
- Shapely legs

Checklist

- **Fabrics:** Soft cottons and linens are good as long as they are not too crisp. Choose fabrics that drape over the body like fine wool jersey knit, wool crepe, and silk. Soft, fine polyester jerseys that skim but do not cling layer well.

- **Pattern:** Subtle shades in solid colors, soft stripes, or medium-sized prints. Muted abstract, swirling designs are a better choice than bold and bright angular patterns.

- **Style elements:** Straight styles with detail at the neckline rather than the bust look good. Plain, cardigan-style jackets layered over tunic tops and straight-cut skirts and pants. Another skirt shape that flatters is the wrap, which gives detail lower in the silhouette, but should be warn with a longer top. Scarves, jewelry, and lovely footwear finish off the styling.

- **Avoid:** Double-breasted jackets and coats, outfits with waist detail, and inappropriately placed pockets. Keep clear of stiff, woven fabric with too much bounce and bright, bold blocks of color.

Choose tunics, long jackets, and dresses that drape over the body.

Choosing the right garment fabric

- Soft woven cotton
- Slinky viscose/rayon knits
- Lightweight knitted fabrics that drape softly
- Wool crepe
- Soft lightweight silks
- Designs with swirls and squiggles in subtle shades
- Paisley prints

These fabric swatches are ideal for the round figure. From top to bottom: Organic print, dobby crepe, voile, and a flowing pattern.

Oval

The oval-shaped figure is above-average height, carrying weight at the waist but with a narrower frame and smaller bust. The added height makes the extra pounds in the middle easy to conceal with long, straight layers and by avoiding any attention at the waist. Rules for an oval-shaped figure are similar to those for the pear shape. Neckline and shoulder details accentuate the upper part of the body, taking the eye up and away from the waist. Raising the waist level alters the proportion and moves the attention away from the middle.

Any feature taking the attention away from the center of the body works for this shape. Keep detail to a minimum at the waist. Belts, elastic, frills, and tops tucked into waistbands are all unsuitable. Layer tops and shirts over the tummy and hide the upper edge of pants and skirts beneath. Choose the length of jackets carefully, taking them lower and to a narrower part of the frame such as the hip or thigh. When selecting styles for a figure with a broad waist, use style details and accessories to focus the eye away from the middle of the body.

Selecting the most flattering styles

Choose unstructured jackets and fine-knit cardigans layered over simple T-shirts and tops. Add width to the shoulders with gathered sleeves. Choose shirts with a collar, or try a V-shaped or wide, embellished neckline. Crisp cotton shirts add volume to the upper half of the body and balance slim-fitting skirts that fall from the middle and glide over the hips. Layer a longer length top or tunic over the skirt where the fabrics meet to detract from the waist.

Pants in all shapes and styles are great for narrow-hipped women. Cropped pants also suit a tall silhouette. Straight and asymmetric skirts work well, and tunic or shift dresses improve the body's proportion. Smock-style garments falling from a yoke are great, providing they are not excessively wide. Accessories and jewelry also help to balance the proportion of the figure by leading the eye to good features and away from a wider waist.

Styles to avoid

Any feature crossing the middle of the body draws attention to this area. Belts, gathered waistbands, short-length jackets, and tucked-in tops are all things to avoid. Wearing loose-fitting, baggy clothing over the tummy adds extra pounds.

The jacket length cuts the body at a slim part of the frame, while the casual, open jacket draws the eye inwards to make the body seem narrower.

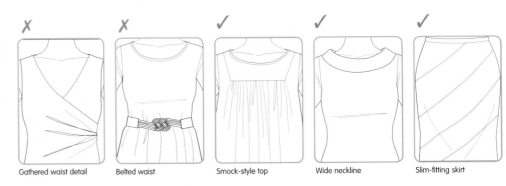

✗	✗	✓	✓	✓
Gathered waist detail	Belted waist	Smock-style top	Wide neckline	Slim-fitting skirt

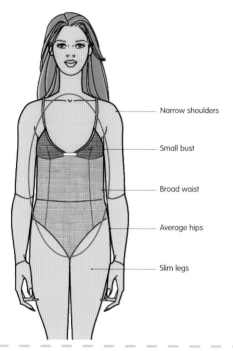

- Narrow shoulders
- Small bust
- Broad waist
- Average hips
- Slim legs

Longer-length jackets and high-waisted dresses flatter an oval shape.

Checklist

- **Fabrics:** Top half: Crisp cotton and linen and light- to medium-weight fabrics worn in layers. Textured fabrics with fancy weaves or added stitch details such as tucks, gathers, and embroidery, structured knitwear, and lightweight jersey/knit.
  Lower half: Wool crepe and soft fabrics for skirts, and the full range of fabrics for pants and jeans.

- **Pattern:** Wear prints, patterns, and stripes printed or woven into the fabric. Choose bold patterns mixed with solids for jackets and cardigans to narrow the frame at the waist.

- **Style elements:** Well-fitting skirts and pants in all styles worn with soft, crisp tops and blouses minimize the waist. Emphasize shoulders and necklines; an open-neck shirt or a rolled collar adds weight to the top of the figure, as do yoke styles with details like tucks, embroidery, or piped seams.

- **Avoid:** Large, shapeless garments should not be worn in an attempt to conceal the waist, since this only enlarges the rest of the body. Steer clear of fabrics with strong horizontal designs worn around the middle, belts, and other waist detailing.

Choosing the right garment fabric

- Denim
- Crisp, woven cottons
- Linen
- Light- and medium-weight silks and satins
- Woolen knits
- Fine woven wool with Spandex

These fabric swatches are ideal for the oval figure. From top to bottom: Embroidered detail, vertical stripes, jersey, printed crepe.

Choosing a pattern

When buying clothes "off the rack" from a store, you can tell instantly if they fit well and suit you. When making your own clothes, however, you need to put more thought into the choice of style and the size you cut out and construct.

There is nothing more disappointing than trying on a garment after hours of sewing to discover that it does not fit and the style does not do justice to your figure. Before you start, take some time to look at yourself in a full-length mirror to recognize your figure type (see pages 20–29) and enlist the help of a friend to give honest advice about your shape.

Having established your silhouette type and the kind of garments to select or avoid, the next vital step is to choose the correct size. Always follow the size chart on the pattern envelope (see pages 40–41) and never assume you will be the same size as garments from a store—this is seldom the case. It is also important to remember that few people fit into a standard size and most of us have figure variations that range between sizes.

After choosing a suitable style in an appropriate size, minor adjustments can be made to achieve a perfect fit.

Where to buy patterns

Pattern catalogs
These thick, glossy books show photographs or illustrations of the finished garments with information on the sizes available and the type and amount of fabric required to create them. Grouped into categories, this makes choosing a suitable outfit easy. They are generally updated with new styles two or four times a year.

Magazines
Some companies publish monthly or quarterly magazines with pull-out patterns and details of how to put the garments together. You can trace these patterns and follow the instructions to create exciting, up-to-date designs in your choice of material.

Downloads
The most obvious advantage of downloading a pattern is that you receive it immediately, but it can take time to print the many parts and even longer to put them together accurately to achieve your pattern pieces.

Checklist: Pattern choice and use

- Select a style that suits you
  (see pages 20–29).
- Choose an appropriate pattern style and size
  (see pages 30–42).
- Make adjustments to the paper pattern
  (see pages 50–134).
- Make a toile to check and adjust the fit
  (see pages 136–153).
- Construct your new garment
  (see pages 156–173).

Printing and assembling a downloaded pattern

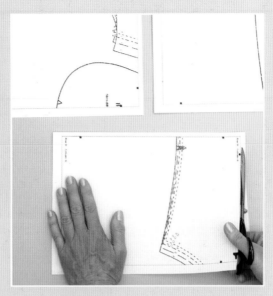

2 First, organize and divide the sheets of paper by rows, numbers, or letters, and cut off the margins on the top and left sides.

1 The downloaded pattern prints on your normal home printer on 8½ x 11 in (21.5 x 28 cm) sheets with a heavy black border. On each sheet are column and row numbers along with small black boxes to help when matching up the sheets.

3 Now you are ready to glue the sheets together side-by-side to form rows. It is important to pay special attention to matching the black boxes. Be as accurate as possible.

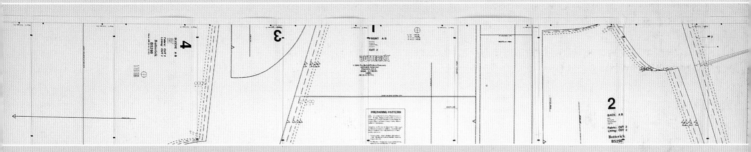

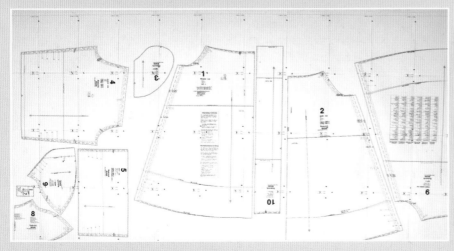

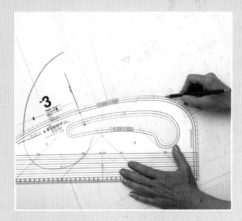

5 Once the pattern is complete, it is a good idea to trace it onto pattern tracing paper. This will make the pattern easier to pin to your fabric because pattern tracing paper is made for that purpose.

4 Once all the rows are finished, paste them together lengthwise. The pattern is now complete.

Pattern envelope information

You will find the essential information you need on the outside of the pattern envelope (before opening it up and fighting with the tissue paper that never seems to go back in the envelope quite the same again!). The pattern information includes advice on the type and quantity of fabric to choose and any other extras you need to buy to complete the piece of clothing illustrated, as well as how to choose the correct size.

Pattern envelope front
The front of the pattern envelope displays the initial vital information to help you select the right pattern for your shape and size.

Photograph or illustration (1 and 2)
The front of the pattern envelope usually shows a photograph or sketch of each item of clothing, complete with variations. This might be a skirt in two or three lengths or a shirt with a choice of collar styles, but all views will be shown, usually from the front. A photograph gives a more realistic idea of how the finished garment will look while an illustration may use a certain amount of artistic license by elongating the model. Always remember your own shape when choosing a pattern and do not be fooled by the elegant model in the illustration, whether a photograph or a sketch.

Size (3)
The size or sizes included in your envelope are stated on the front and a chart is often printed on the flap of the envelope, though sometimes this information is contained inside the envelope. Generally there will be a range of at least three sizes offered by the pattern, but some multi-size patterns may include 10 or 12 options. Make sure you buy the pattern in the size range that best covers your measurements.

Pattern number (4)
This identifies each pattern, making it easy to order your selection.

Illustration (2)

Pattern number (4)

Sizes (3)

Photograph (1)

The maximum size of the pattern

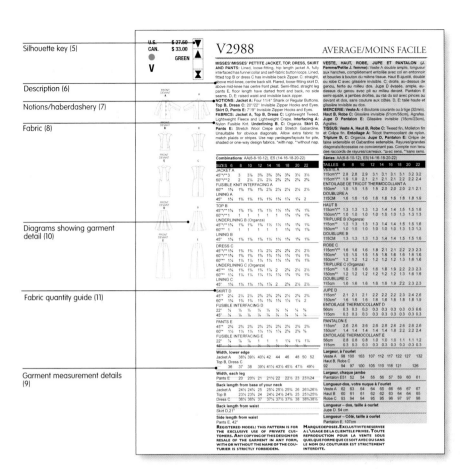

Silhouette key (5)

Description (6)

Notions/haberdashery (7)

Fabric (8)

Diagrams showing garment detail (10)

Fabric quantity guide (11)

Garment measurement details (9)

The pattern envelope

The back of the envelope carries a lot of essential information, including how to calculate the amount of fabric you will need.

Pattern envelope back

On the back of the pattern envelope you will find detailed information about your pattern.

Silhouette key (5)

Some companies suggest the figure types a garment style is suitable for by using a very simple key of triangles and rectangles. This supports the knowledge you have of your own figure (see pages 20–29) and helps with pattern selection.

Description (6)

A short written description of each item of clothing is given with details such as how it should fit, whether a lining is included, and information about fastenings. This, in addition to the outline view and main illustration, will give a complete vision of the finished garments.

Notions/haberdashery (7)

This is where the extra requirements needed to complete each garment are included. If a zipper is necessary, it will state the length and type, or the number and size of buttons required. Lining and underlining requirements are also listed.

Fabric (8)

Information about suitable fabrics is always included to help you to choose appropriately. This will suggest the weight or stretch required for a good fit. You may already have a fabric in mind and this will confirm its suitability or make you aware of other aspects of the design you had not considered.

Garment measurement details (9)

Measurements of the completed garments are included to help you to visualize how the finished item will look. For example, the skirt length, or the hem circumference on a pair of pants, are useful pieces of information to know before buying a pattern. These details are not always evident from the outline diagrams or illustrations, and this allows you to choose or reject a particular pattern or be aware that alterations will be required to achieve the look you want.

Diagrams showing garment detail (10)

The front and back views of each item included in the pattern envelope are illustrated, showing seam and dart positions and fastenings. This adds to the visual information given in the photograph or sketch on the envelope front.

Fabric quantity guide (11)

As well as offering suggestions for choosing suitable fabric, charts are also included to show how much you need to buy for each view and size. Since fabric can be bought in a range of widths, following this chart will help you to avoid buying too little or too much material.

Inside the pattern envelope

Inside the pattern envelope, you will find information pages to guide you through the construction of your new garment. Sheets of tissue paper with the pattern pieces printed on one side are included and will need to be prepared before use.

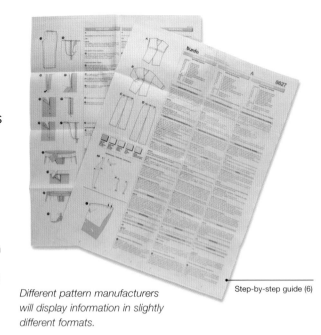

Pattern instructions

Having chosen suitable fabric and haberdashery items, the next step is to read the information pages to gain an overview of the steps to creating your new garment. It is a good idea to check over all the stages of construction before cutting into your fabric. The instructions show how to lay out the pattern pieces and cut out the fabric both economically and to give the best finish. After this, step-by-step instructions advise on the order of construction and the techniques involved in combining the fabric pieces. When you are satisfied with the information gleaned from the pattern, it is time to get started.

Different pattern manufacturers will display information in slightly different formats.

Step-by-step guide (6)

Line drawings (1)

Line drawings show details of the finished items included in the pattern with a number or letter to indicate the view you plan to follow. The pattern pieces may look similar to each other, so this helps to differentiate between, for example, a knee-length or a calf-length skirt.

Pattern pieces (2)

All the pattern pieces are listed or shown as small-scale diagrams and are numbered to make it easy to identify them when cutting and selecting the tissue pieces.

Measurement chart (3)

This is often included on the instruction sheet but may be printed on the tissue itself. It helps to identify the correct size you need to cut out. (See pages 40–41 for advice on selecting the most appropriate size). Some indicate how and where to take your body measurements.

Fabric cutting layouts (4)

Various layout options are given as a guide to how to best fit the pattern pieces on the fabric, depending on the width of the cloth and the view you've chosen. This may also include interfacing, underlining, and lining.

Information key (5)

A key is also included to make sense of the layout guide, indicating the right and wrong sides of the fabric and whether lining or interfacing have to be cut out, too.

Step-by-step guide (6)

Brief instructions provide the necessary information, along with diagrams, to make each step clear and comprehensive. Some basic sewing knowledge is required, but these instructions are all that is needed to construct the garment, providing they are followed carefully and in order.

Preparing the pattern

1 Identify the pattern pieces required to create the garment and cut these away from the others. Put the remaining pieces back in the envelope.

2 If necessary, iron the tissue paper to flatten it and to remove any folds or creases before cutting. Use a warm, dry iron.

Line drawings (1)   Measurement chart (3)   Fabric cutting layouts (4)

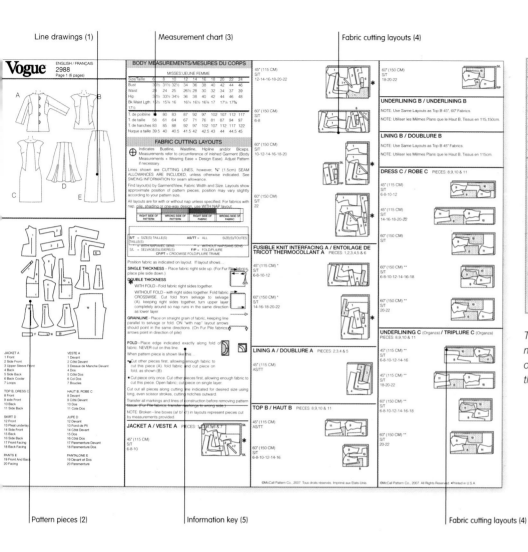

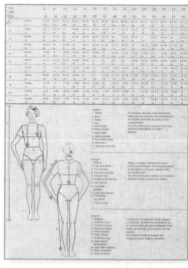

The size chart details the average measurements of the figure for a range of sizes. See page 40 for how to use this chart.

Pattern pieces (2)   Information key (5)   Fabric cutting layouts (4)

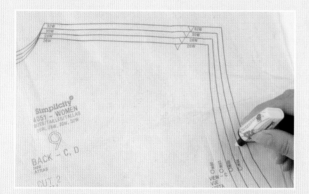

3 Identify the cutting line for your size with a highlighter on all pattern pieces.

4 Cut all pattern pieces in the appropriate size and arrange on the fabric.

Note: If you have any pattern adjustments to make, such as altering the length, do this before laying the pieces on the fabric.

Understanding the pattern

The symbols printed on the pattern pieces may seem like an elaborate code, but this shorthand is easy to follow when you know how to decipher the shapes and marks.

What it all means

Commercial pattern companies tend to use the same symbols and so it should only take a short time to learn what the information means and how to use it. Once you can recognize the message given by each printed shape or mark and how to use it, you can sew with any pattern easily. Some of these symbols help in laying out the pattern on the fabric, while others need to be transferred to the fabric to accurately match pieces later in the construction.

Pattern number (1)

Each pattern piece shows the company that produced it and includes a number identifying it from all other patterns.

Part number and description (2)

Each piece will be named and have a number indicating its part in the finished garment, e.g. front, collar, sleeve, pocket, etc.

Number of pieces (3)

Information will be included to state how many pieces you should cut out in fabric, lining, and/or interfacing.

Shortening/lengthening lines (4)

A double line drawn horizontally through a pattern piece shows where it is best to shorten or lengthen a garment to achieve an appropriate length.

Balance marks (5)

Dots and spots printed on a paper pattern are important in helping to place the fabric panels together. These are often used for marking dart or tuck positions and should be transferred with tailor's tacks (see page 38).

Cutting lines (6)

Traditionally, patterns were produced for individual sizes and the cutting line was indicated with a solid line and the sewing line by a dotted line. On most patterns today, where several size options are included, a range of lines is used to identify different sizes and the sewing line is assumed to be a seam allowance width inside this. Work out which line is used for your size (dots, dashes, solid, etc.) then cut along these lines for each pattern piece.

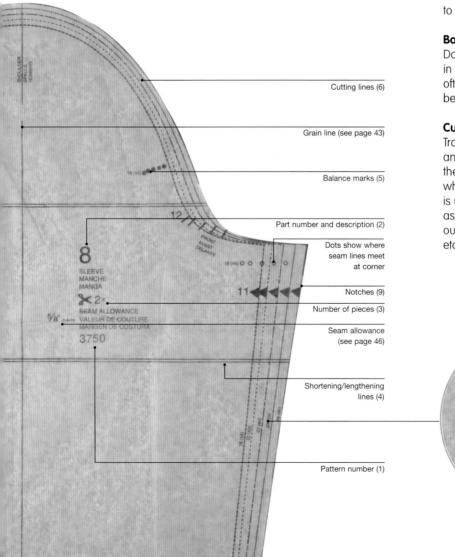

- Cutting lines (6)
- Grain line (see page 43)
- Balance marks (5)
- Part number and description (2)
- Dots show where seam lines meet at corner
- Notches (9)
- Number of pieces (3)
- Seam allowance (see page 46)
- Shortening/lengthening lines (4)
- Pattern number (1)

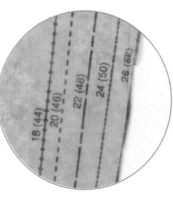

Each size is identified with a different style of cutting line. These are not necessarily the same for every pattern so check your size before cutting.

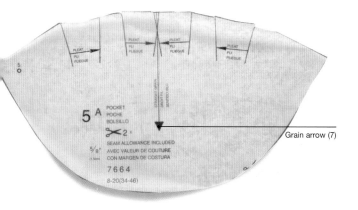

Grain arrow (7)

Grain arrows (7)

Arrows printed on paper patterns show the direction the grain of the fabric should lie in when cutting out the pieces. This line must be parallel to the selvage edge (see page 43) for the finished garment to hang correctly.

Curved arrows (8)

An arrow with curved ends pointing to a solid line indicates that the pattern piece should be placed against a fold. This ensures the fabric piece will be perfectly symmetrical when laid out and is often used for the back of a jacket or the front of a skirt where there is no seam.

Notches (9)

Notches are used on the cutting lines to show where fabric pieces will be joined together. This helps to ensure that skirt panels are put together correctly and longer, shaped seams can be eased together in the right place; for example, through the bust point of a princess seam. Similarly, when sewing a sleeve into an armhole, single (front) and double (back) notches are generally used so that the arms are inserted in the correct armholes.

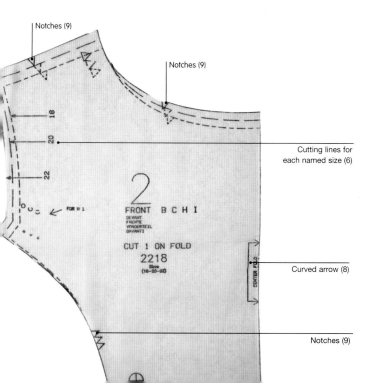

Notches (9)

Notches (9)

Cutting lines for each named size (6)

Curved arrow (8)

Notches (9)

Using notches

When laying the pattern pieces on the fabric, cut around the notches to help match seams together. It is better to cut around these than snip into the seam allowance as this avoids weakening the seam.

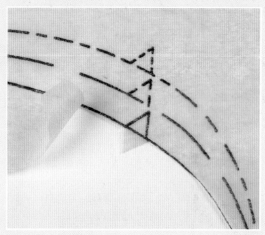

Cutting around a notch
Cut notches "out" rather than "in" to prevent weakening the seam.

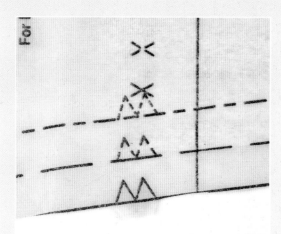

Matching up notches
Make sure you link up double notches with the corresponding double notch, and likewise with single notches.

Transferring pattern markings

Some important points must be accurately transferred from the paper pattern onto the fabric. This can be done using a number of methods, including tailor's tacks, temporary markers (chalk or pens), or pins.

Tailor's chalk and temporary pens

Use this method if tailor's chalk or a wash-away or fade-away pen will show up on the material.

1 Place a pin straight through the pattern marking and through the fabric layers.

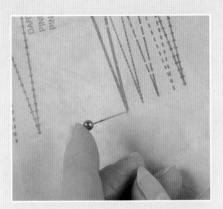

Tailor's tacks

Use tailor's tacks for balance points and darts. Use basting thread or thread of a contrasting color.

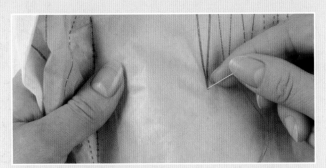

1 Thread a needle and place this into the pattern marking and through the two layers of fabric underneath.

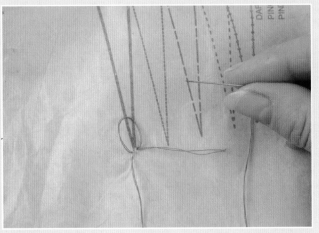

2 Bring the needle back to the right side and repeat, leaving a loose loop on the surface. Cut the thread end.

3 Ease the fabric pieces apart and snip between them.

4 Threads are left on both pieces of fabric to use as temporary marking positions.

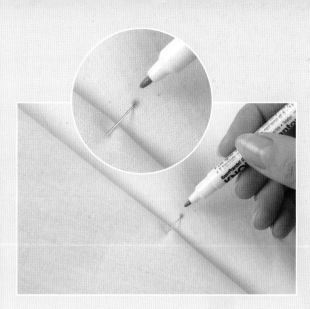

2 Carefully separate the layers of fabric and mark the pin position with chalk or a temporary pen on both sides.

3 Remove the pin; both layers are now marked.

Pins

This is a suitable method if sewing is going to take place immediately. It is ideal for darts.

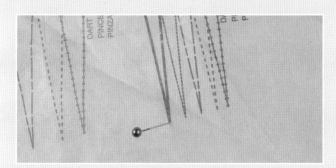

1 Place a pin straight through the pattern marking.

2 Pick up both layers of fabric and place a pin through the same position from the opposite side.

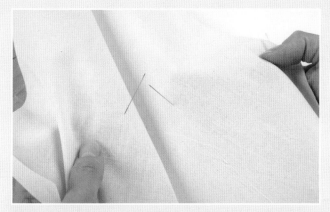

3 Ease the two fabric layers apart so that the pins separate and each sticks through a single layer.

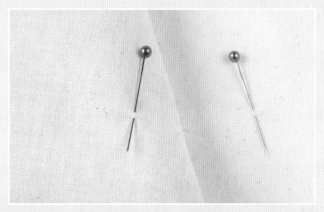

4 Reposition the pins so they sit securely in the fabric to indicate the positions of the markings until required.

Size charts and measurements

Choosing the best size is vital to achieve a good fit, which can be very tricky.

Measure accurately

Stand in front of a full-length mirror while you, or a friend, take your body measurements. Keep the tape measure parallel to the floor for horizontal measurements and make sure the tape is flat with no twists. Keep the tape measure snug but not tight, and remember to breathe.

Photocopy this

Write all your measurements down and remember to re-measure if your body changes shape over time.

Measurement chart

Landmark	Standard measurements	Personal measurements
1 Bust		
2 Waist		
3 Hip		
4 Chest		
5 Back width		
6 Shoulder		
7 Upper arm		
8 Wrist		
9 Height		
10 Nape to waist		
11 Shoulder to front waist		
12 Arm length		
13 Waist to hip		
14 Waist to floor		
15 Waist to knee		
16 Crotch depth		

Record your measurements

Photocopy the chart provided here and write down all your measurements in the right-hand column. Use the diagrams on page 19 to help you know where to take your body measurements. Compare your measurements with those given by the pattern company. These can be found on the outside of the envelope, but they are sometimes printed on the tissue paper inside. Decide the size you are closest to and write those measurements down in the left column. Highlight any anomalies (for example, bust measurement or back length) and be aware of these when cutting out and adapting your paper pattern.

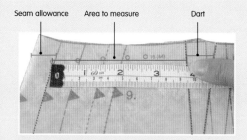
Seam allowance | Area to measure | Dart

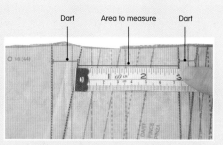
Dart | Area to measure | Dart

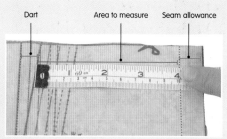
Dart | Area to measure | Seam allowance

Measure the pattern pieces

Check your measurements against the actual pattern before deciding which size to cut out. To do this, select the relevant pattern pieces and measure the actual size of the pattern without seam allowances and darts. Ease will be included (see page 46) so bear this in mind and compare the pattern size with your measurement.

Choose your size

Make a decision about the size that best suits you and cut out the tissue paper. If you need to adapt the pattern, do this now (see pages 50–133).

As a general rule, choose skirts and pants using your hip measurement, and tops and jackets with your bust measurement in mind. However, this is not always the case and it is important to have a feeling for your general build. For example, if you have a small frame yet a large bust, using this measurement will result in a garment that may fit at the bust but will be too big elsewhere. Here, use the measurements based on your shoulders, back, and chest, and make a bust enlargement to the pattern.

Multi-size patterns

Patterns normally offer a choice of sizes, making it easier to create a well-fitting garment for a variety of figures. This may be three or four sizes, although some multi-patterns offer a much larger range.

The advantage of such a large size range is that it makes it possible to buy just one pattern and to choose the cutting lines to achieve a good fit. For example, a typical pear shape may require a size 20 top and 26 skirt, so with a multi-size pattern a well-fitting dress can be created. Since most of us are of a non-standard size, we can use the pattern lines to create an individual fit from a commercial paper pattern.

Using a multi-size pattern

1 Mark your own measurements onto the size chart and take note of where they lie in relation to the standard measurements. Make a decision on the size or sizes required. If one of the measurements appears as an anomaly, the pattern will need to be adjusted separately in this area.

2 Find the relevant pattern pieces and lay them out flat, noting the cutting line key for the size or sizes needed (see page 36).

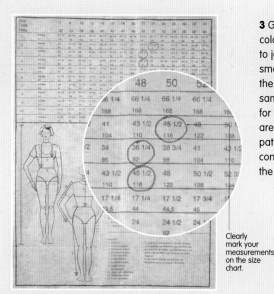

Clearly mark your measurements on the size chart.

3 Go over the cutting lines required with a colored pen or pencil and draw new lines to join or merge between sizes, creating a smooth line. Where seams join, make sure the lines on both pattern pieces follow the same angle. A French curve is a useful tool for this task (see page 9). When the lines are completed, cut out the pattern pieces and continue with the construction.

Fabric preparation

With the pattern cut and ready to use, it is time to consider your fabric.

The information on the outside of the pattern will have informed you of the material suitable for your garment and how much of it to buy, but now you need to check for flaws and preshrink it in preparation for cutting. Many factors influence how to prepare the fabric, such as fiber content, construction, and the type of outfit being made.

Fabric construction

Most of the fabrics that we use for clothes are either woven or knitted. These handle differently and so are used for different purposes. A woven fabric is fairly stable and will only stretch if pulled diagonally along the cross or bias grain, while a knitted fabric will stretch in at least one direction when pulled because of its loopy structure. This is why it is important to follow the guidelines given for fabric choice, since the drape or fit will depend on the fabric formation.

Checking for flaws

It is unlikely that the fabric you buy will have anything wrong with it, but check it first, just in case. A good way to check for pulled threads or print mistakes is to iron the entire length of cloth before laying it out for cutting. This allows you to check the surface of the cloth, and in addition, ironing it with a steam iron will help to preshrink the fabric. If you do find any problems with the material, you can either take this up with the retailer or work around any minor imperfections.

Preshrinking

Most fabric is sold with a small shrinkage allowance, and for peace of mind you should prelaunder the length of fabric before cutting out your garment. The steam-ironing method, mentioned above, may suffice for some fabrics and is a perfect way of testing clothing that will be dry-cleaned. Where you will be combining different fabrics, for example, one with a lining or those embellished with laces or trims, prelaundering is recommended. To prelaunder the fabric, just launder it as directed by the fabric manufacturer. If this information is not available, treat it as you intend to wash the finished garment.

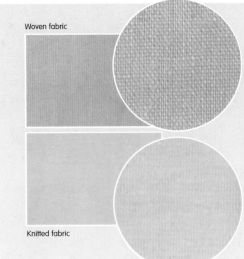

Woven fabric

Knitted fabric

Fabric

Fabric is most commonly made by weaving or knitting yarns or threads together. The threads in a woven fabric lie at 90 degrees to each other. Knitted fabric is produced by interlocking loops of threads.

Cutting a straight end on woven cloth

To cut a length of fabric across the grain and achieve a perfectly straight line, pull out one thread from the weft, i.e. the threads across the length and not parallel to the selvage. As you pull out a single thread, the fabric will crinkle and, if it pulls free without breaking, a line will be obvious through the fabric. Cut along this line.

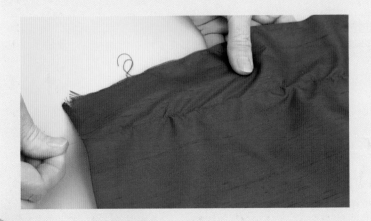

Squaring up skewed fabric
Sometimes you will find your fabric length has been pulled off-grain, giving a slight diamond shape rather than a regular rectangle. If this is the case, ease the fabric back into shape by pulling diagonally in the opposite direction to rectify the problem. Finish by pressing with an iron and lying flat to cool.

Laying out fabric

It is important to plan the layout of the pattern pieces on fabric carefully.

Fabrics are normally laid out with the selvage edges placed together so that two fronts, backs, or sleeves can be cut out together and will therefore be identical. However, in certain circumstances it is better to lay the fabric in a single layer, turning and reusing the pattern templates to cut more than one panel. Use a single layer when cutting a bold pattern or checks to make matching easier or if the fabric is particularly slinky or slippery. Cut the latter on a cotton sheet to prevent the fabric from sliding off the table.

The layout options given in the pattern envelope will include suggestions of how to place the pattern pieces according to the width of the fabric and whether the material has a nap or direction. Follow the directions given until you have sufficient experience to be able to create your own best layouts.

Fabric direction

Some fabrics will have "direction." This may be due to a design or print with an obvious top and bottom or a surface nap or pile that is brushed in a particular direction, such as flannel or velvet. When laying out the fabric, it is important to place all the pattern pieces in the same direction, otherwise shade differences may be apparent or flowers may be upside down.

Printed directional fabric
Cut all pieces in the same direction.

Pile fabric
When cut in opposite directions, shading differences are obvious.

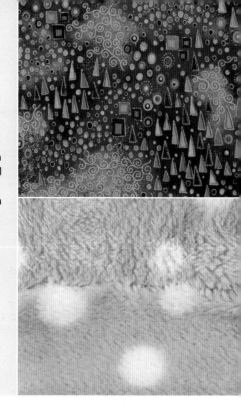

Finding the right side of the fabric

The surface of a fabric is sometimes obvious, but the right and reverse sides may appear very similar. To work out which side is intended to be the right side, look for tiny holes running along the selvages of the fabric. This is where the fabric was supported during processing with "tentering" hooks. If you run your finger over the holes, one side will be smooth and the other rough. The rough side is the right side, as the hooks are placed through the material from the wrong side so the edge of the hole is pushed to the surface.

Useful fabric terms

Selvage This is the narrow, heavier band that runs down both sides of a length of fabric. It is where the weft (filling) threads have wrapped around the edge of the warp (lengthwise) threads and returned to be woven in the opposite direction.

Warp These are the lengthwise threads that are placed on the loom first to form the basis of the fabric.

Weft These are the filling threads that weave up and down through the warp threads to create the cloth.

Grain The grain of a fabric follows the length and is parallel to the selvage edges. When placing pattern pieces on fabric, the grain arrows must lie parallel to the selvage for the garment to hang properly.

Bias The true bias or true cross lies at 45 degrees to the warp and weft. The fabric is unstable when pulled in this direction, as it does not follow the grain. However, this can be an advantage if a draping effect is required, because clothes hang softly when cut this way. Bias binding is cut on the bias to prevent crinkles and unsightly tucks when covering a shaped edge.

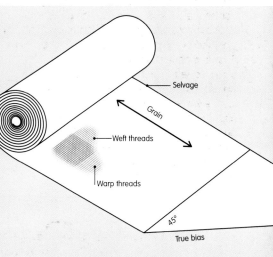

Positioning patterns on different fabrics

It is important to carefully consider how pattern pieces are placed onto fabric. If some of the pieces are positioned slightly off the grain, the resulting drape or hang of the finished garment may appear twisted. Some types of cloth require all of the pattern pieces to lie in a consistent direction, while this is not necessary for other materials. When working with bold prints or distinctive stripes or checks it is essential to match the pattern at the seams. Follow the information provided in the pattern instructions to avoid unnecessary mistakes.

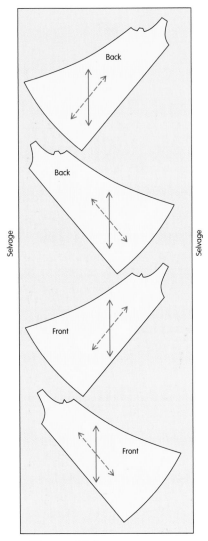

Bias-cut fabric

When an elegant drape is required, the pattern pieces are positioned at 45° to the grain. Use the original grain arrow (dotted) and draw a new one. For best results cut the pieces singly, turning the pattern over to cut left and right halves.

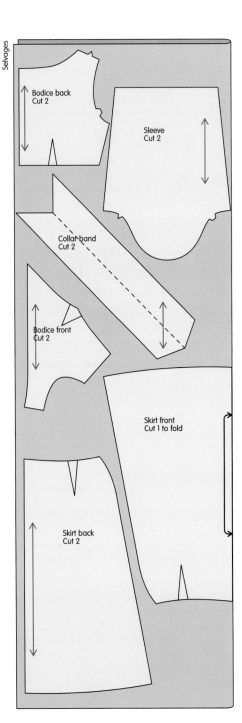

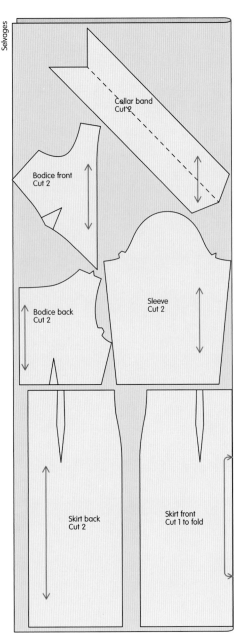

Fabric with a pile or nap

If a fabric has a pile or a one-way pattern, all of the pieces must be laid in the same direction; otherwise, some panels may appear different when the garment is finished.

Plain fabric

Plain fabric with no nap, pile, or direction. Pieces can be dovetailed to make best use of the fabric, providing the grain arrows are followed.

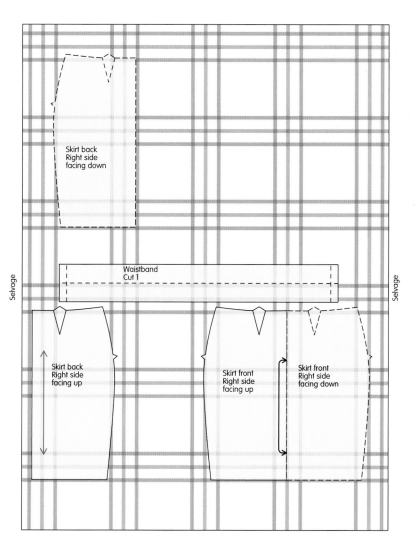

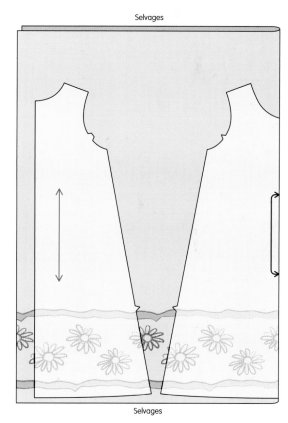

Checked fabric

Where there is a distinct pattern of stripes, checks, or plaids, it is important that the pattern pieces are placed on the fabric carefully to ensure that the seams match. Cut out singly and use the notches and balance points as markers to help with seam matching. Remember to match at the seam line, not the cutting line.

Note: When cutting out pieces on a single layer of fabric, cut one pattern piece with the right side up and one reversed so that symmetrical left and right pieces are cut (not two lefts or two rights).

Border print

Sometimes fabric is printed with a border along one edge. To take advantage of the design, open the fabric out, then refold the material so that the border lies on one edge. Make sure the border will match at the seams and place the grain arrows parallel to the folded edge rather than at the selvages.

Allowances and ease

When patterns are drafted, they include extra fabric so that the garments are comfortable to wear and do not restrict movement. There is also additional material added at the seams and hems so that the fabric panels can be joined together and the edges can be finished appropriately.

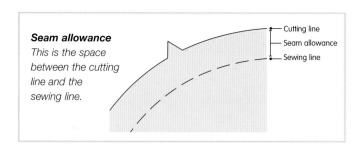

Seam allowance
This is the space between the cutting line and the sewing line.

- Cutting line
- Seam allowance
- Sewing line

Seam allowances

An "allowance" is the term given to the border added to the edge of a pattern between the cutting line and the sewing line so that the fabric pieces can be sewn together and the edges folded and finished. This means that the pieces are joined on the actual fitting line and the excess can be used to give a tidy finish on the inside. Most pattern companies include seam and hem allowances in their patterns to enable you to piece together the panels and finish the edges. However, sometimes these are omitted and you can add the allowances you wish to use. Before cutting any fabric make sure you know whether or not these allowances are included or need to be added. Standard seam allowances for home sewing are generally ⅝ in (1.5 cm), although in the garment making industry ⅜ in (1 cm) seam allowances are used. A 1 in (2.5 cm) seam allowance is commonly used when creating couture garments for neat zipper insertion and easier fitting.

Patterns with no seam allowances included

There are companies, such as Burda, that produce some patterns without any seam or hem allowances added to the pieces. This makes it easier to manipulate parts of the pattern by moving darts or altering the style before cutting out the fabric. Without the seam allowances, this adaptation is more accurate and the allowances you choose to use can be added after these changes have been made so that the fabric panels can be joined together. These patterns are useful as a starting point when making style

alterations, although it is also possible to use patterns that include seam allowances.

Ease

In addition to extra allowances being included for piecing panels together, "ease" is also incorporated into a design. This is the amount of excess fullness allowed for movement in a design for comfort (wearing ease) as well as style (design ease) and ranges from none in bra making and swimwear to several inches in coats. The correct amount of ease is critical to the comfort and look of a finished garment. Seasonal fashion has a great influence on ease and there have been phases through the years where oversized garments were popular while at other times a close-fitting silhouette is the style everyone is after. Garments made from knitted cloth do not require as much ease as those made from woven material, as the fabric moves with the body rather than constricting it. Because of this, a sewing pattern will state whether or not it is designed for stretch fabric.

To ensure that you achieve the look you want, always take note of the ease included in a garment or the finished measurements on the back of a pattern envelope, as this helps to indicate the amount of ease included. Some patterns also describe the fit of a garment by classifying it as close-fitting, fitted, semi-fitted, loose-fitting, or very loose-fitting. This means that you may well fit into a dress two sizes smaller than you really are, but it will not look the way the designer intended it to.

Hems

The amount of extra fabric added for a hem depends on the shape of the hem and the type of garment. Suggested hem depths have been included here, but they are only a guide.

Straight hem
A straight edge can take a deep hem (1½–2 in/3.2–5 cm) as it does not need to be manipulated into place. The fabric in a deep hem adds weight and helps the garment to hang well. This would be suitable for a skirt made up of rectangular panels gathered at the waist.

Hem with tucks
In the hem (1¼ in/1.2 cm) of a curved A-line or circular skirt the raw edge is longer than the finished edge will be, so extra fabric has to be tucked or folded away to fit into place. A deep hem like this causes extra bulk, so it would be better to find an alternative such as a narrow or faced hem.

Tips for assessing built-in ease

Always check the information on the pattern for clues to the fit and the amount of ease built into a piece of clothing. This way, you will create the most appropriate size that will give you the best possible look.

- The actual dimensions of a garment are sometimes stated on the pattern envelope or tissue; for example, bust, hip, or hem circumference. Alternatively, the information may be given as an "ease" measurement. Both these methods enable you to compare the actual sizing to your own body.
- A further indication of the amount of ease incorporated into a design can be seen on the photograph on the front of the envelope, as this shows how the garment is intended to be worn.

However, if there is an illustration rather than a photograph this is less useful as it may not tell the full story.

- Measure the actual pattern pieces across the bust, waist, and hip and remove the seam allowances. Place the tape measure, set at this measurement, around the appropriate part of the body to see how much "space" is incorporated into the design. This will help you to visualize how the finished garment will look on you.
- Take care when using old patterns because styles and outlines change and the amount of ease will alter from decade to decade. The general style and features of a pattern may appear to be what is required, but excess ease may give a completely different look than the one you'd hoped for.

Garment types
Some patterns will use these categories to classify a garment.

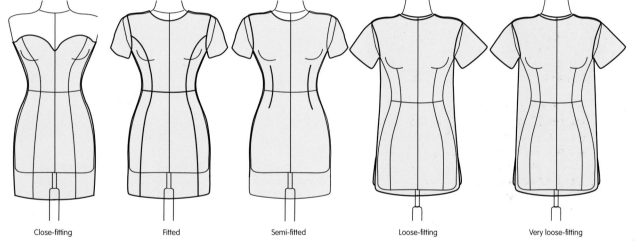

Close-fitting   Fitted   Semi-fitted   Loose-fitting   Very loose-fitting

Narrow curved hem
A narrow hem (¼ in/6 mm) is a good option on a curved edge. This could be sewn by hand, stitched with a hemmer foot on a sewing machine, or serged to give a rolled hem (see page 10).

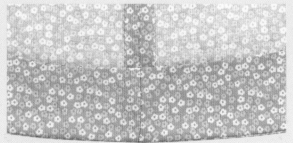

Faced hem
When a deep hem of 3 in (7.5 cm) is needed to add weight to the lower edge but the hem is shaped (for example on a wedding gown) a faced hem is the best option. This is cut separately as a shaped piece and sewn to the hem (see page 160).

Adapting patterns

This section offers advice on how to adapt a commercial pattern to improve the fit. By folding and tucking, cutting and spreading patterns, or altering darts a much better fit will be achieved.

Fit issues to look out for

We all have figure variations, not figure problems! The problems only arise when we try to achieve a good fit from a standard pattern using measurements that are not our own. However, with a little knowledge of pattern adjustment, these issues are easy to overcome.

Common areas for adjustment
Providing you measure accurately and start with the best-fitting pattern, you will only need to make minor adjustments. The most common areas requiring adjustment are highlighted here.

Shoulder (see pages 55–61)
Shoulder length varies from one person to the next. A jacket, for example, may look too big or too small as a result, even if every other part of the jacket fits well. By comparing your shoulder length with the pattern before cutting it out, you will save a great deal of time and effort at a later stage.

Neckline (see pages 62–69)
There are so many different neckline styles that, very often, gaping and tight neckline problems can be addressed by simply choosing a design to suit your figure. Where a neckline or collar does not sit comfortably on the neck and chest, attention to posture may be the answer. If bad posture is not the problem, simple changes to the shoulder of the pattern can improve how a collar or neckline lies.

Bust (see pages 70–85)
This part of the body causes more fitting troubles than any other, but by choosing an appropriate pattern size for the basic frame and adapting the bust area, a much better fit can be achieved. Follow our step-by-step instructions and feel the difference in your new clothes.

Hollow back (see page 104)
A hollow back is a common complaint. This makes it difficult to get pants and skirts to fit comfortably at the waist because the fabric sits away from the body or lies far below the waistline. Recutting the pattern, adjusting the darts, and even using an alternative waist style will noticeably improve the fit.

Sleeve length (see pages 89–90)
Adjusting sleeve length is a simple matter and requires only shortening or lengthening of the pattern piece before cutting out the fabric. If you have shorter-than-average arms, make a tuck in the sleeve pattern to allow for this. Move the pattern pieces apart if you need to lengthen the sleeve.

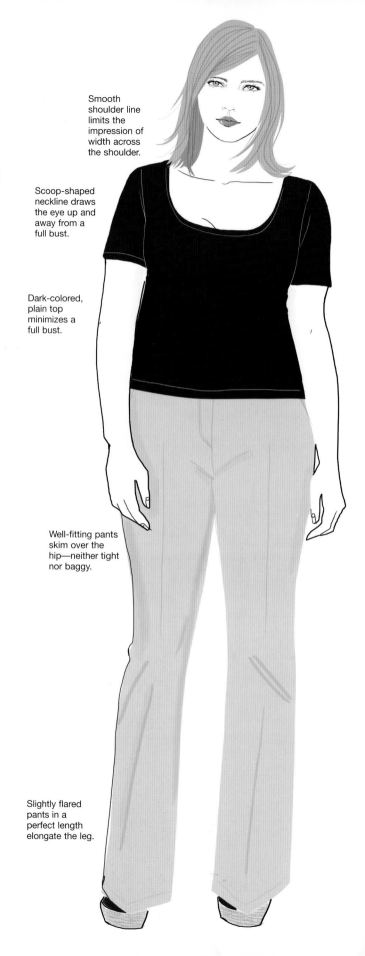

Smooth shoulder line limits the impression of width across the shoulder.

Scoop-shaped neckline draws the eye up and away from a full bust.

Dark-colored, plain top minimizes a full bust.

Well-fitting pants skim over the hip—neither tight nor baggy.

Slightly flared pants in a perfect length elongate the leg.

Wide neckline provides more width across the shoulder to help balance with the lower half of the body.

Short sleeve helps to broaden the body at bust level.

The asymmetric gathering draws attention to a narrow waist.

Appropriate dress length cuts the leg at the most flattering level.

Armhole (see pages 98–100)
Gaping armholes, with or without a fitted sleeve, will make a dress, blouse, or jacket look too big, and in the case of a sleeveless garment, may expose more flesh than desired. Conversely, an armhole that is too small may rub on the skin, making it uncomfortable to wear. Adjustments made to the bodice pattern will ensure a good fit when finished.

Waist (see pages 101–103)
A skirt or dress with a poorly fitting waist can be irritating or uncomfortable to wear. By manipulating darts and seams on the pattern before cutting, it is easy to accomplish a comfortable waist that looks good too.

Hip (see pages 105–109)
Whether full or narrow, this part of the pattern often requires an alteration for a smooth silhouette that follows the shape of the hip (neither pulling nor hanging away from the body). Changing the dart length or modifying the side seam shaping will improve the fit of pants, skirts, and dresses over the hip.

Stomach (see pages 110–111)
A large stomach may create stress in the side seams of a skirt or dress and cause the hem to be uneven, as the fabric sits high on the waist and falls over the tummy. With pants, this can make the crotch ride up and feel uncomfortable. By enlarging the front pattern pieces, a much improved and more comfortable fit will be realized.

Bottom (see pages 112–115)
Simple adjustments to a pattern will allow for a protruding or a flat bottom to be accommodated by a garment. Excess fabric can be lost and extra fabric added to a back pattern piece to achieve a good fit in a skirt, dress, or pair of pants.

Crotch depth (see pages 120–122)
A poorly fitting pair of pants can be either very uncomfortable or just unflattering. Either way, a good fit is a must and can be achieved by reshaping the front and back leg pattern pieces before cutting out the fabric.

Height (see pages 127–131)
This is the easiest of all adjustments to make, and simply involves tucking or cutting and lengthening the pattern in the appropriate places. If you have a long back, you will need to add extra length in the front and back bodice pieces, while someone with long legs will need to extend the skirt or pant pattern pieces.

Altering patterns: Dos and don'ts

It is easy to fall into some obvious traps when making pattern alterations. Knowing how to avoid them is the secret of achieving a perfectly fitted look. If you take your time and follow some basic rules, you'll get a professional finish every time.

✗ The shoulders are too big and the cuffs are too long.

✗ The shoulders are too big, but the cuffs are the correct length.

✓ The shoulders and cuffs are now correctly proportioned.

Shortening sleeves on a jacket

It is important to look at the whole garment before making a judgment about an alteration. A good example of this is sleeve length. If your sleeves are too long and hide your fingers, this will make a jacket look as if it is too big for you. However, the problem may be that you have narrow shoulders while the sleeve length is fine. In this case, the jacket will still look too large if the hem is shortened at the cuff. A shoulder adjustment would be the best solution.

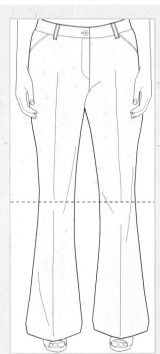

✗ Length has been added to the bottom of the flare without continuing flare angle so it appears straight. The knee position is too high.

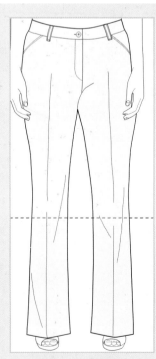

✗ The flare has been shortened due to the adjustment at the hem. The knee position is too low.

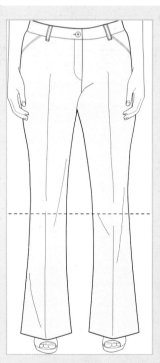

✓ The flare is well proportioned here as the pattern was adjusted from the middle of the leg. The knee position is correct.

Adjusting the length of pants

How difficult can it be to make a pair of pants longer or shorter—just add a few extra inches to the base or chop off the excess at the bottom of the pattern and cut out the fabric? No one would ever know they weren't made for you! However, shortening flared or boot-cut pants from the hem will distort the balance, putting the knee in the wrong place and altering the overall proportion. For a professional finish, the pattern should be shortened from the middle of the leg, before the fabric is cut out, to maintain the balance.

✗ The center panel is too wide.

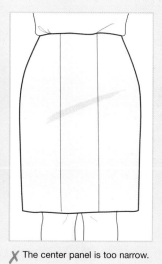

✗ The center panel is too narrow.

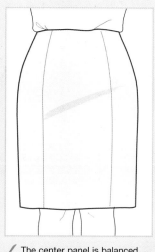

✓ The center panel is balanced.

Making a skirt wider

Making a skirt wider to fit around your hips and bottom does not just involve adding inches to the side seams or placing the front panel away from the fold when you cut it. This simply results in distorting the balance of the panels and may even give the illusion that you are wider than you really are. For balanced panels, decide how many inches or centimeters must be added for the skirt to fit and divide the amount evenly between all the panels so that each is made proportionately bigger.

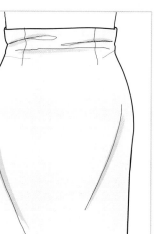

Altering length

As commercial sewing patterns are based on standard measurements, a size 20 dress will be expected to fit a woman of 5 ft 1 in (155 cm) and also her friend who might be 5 ft 11 in (183 cm) tall. They might be completely different shapes but still want to look good in the same style. With a bit of "tucking and folding" or "cutting and extending" of the pattern in the correct places, this is possible.

Fine-tuning darts

Sometimes major alterations are made to a pattern when a simple change in the angle or length of a dart would work instead. An hourglass-shaped model wearing a skirt with waist darts that are too long will find her skirt rising up over her stomach and hips. This is because the darts reduce the skirt circumference in the wrong place; by shortening them the skirt will sit at the correct level around the hips.

Adjusting pattern length keeps a dress in proportion whether you are tall or short.

Bust, waist, and hip levels are all in the correct positions on both models.

Rules for altering patterns

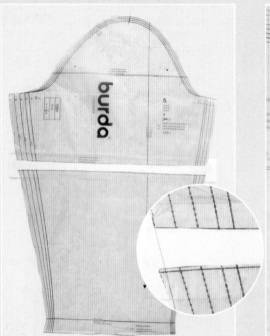

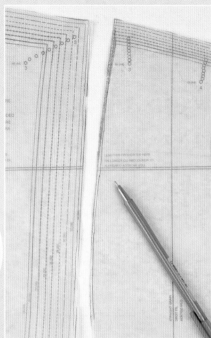

Multi-size patterns

Multi-size patterns make altering the fit
so much easier because they give you
guidelines to follow. They are especially
useful for women who differ in size for
tops and bottoms. It is easy to graduate
from one cutting line to another for a
smooth finish. Make use of the cutting
lines, but do be aware that joining two
very different sizes may look wrong,
and further adjustments or even a
change of style may be necessary.

Reshaping seam lines

After making a pattern adjustment, remember
to redraw the seam lines for a smooth finish,
for example when shortening or lengthening
a pattern, as a little gap is left in the seam.
Simply redraw the cutting lines before the
fabric is cut out for a flat seam finish.

Keeping panels balanced

Make sure you apply small measurement
changes to all the relevant seams rather than
one large amount to a single seam. This helps
to keep the proportion of a garment balanced,
illustrated perfectly by a dress with princess
seams, where additions only to the side seams
would make the center panel appear
unnaturally narrow.

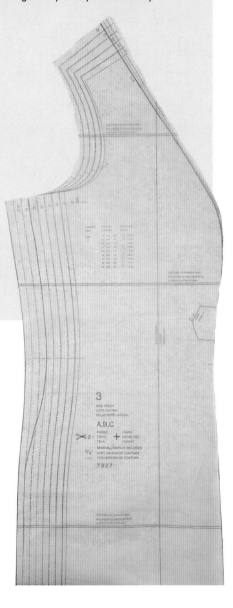

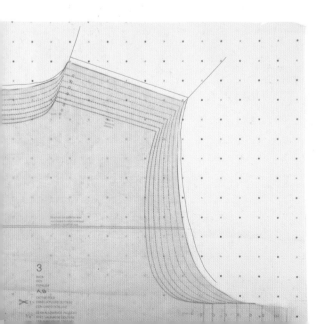

Grading

*Sometimes it is necessary to resize
a pattern beyond the largest size
shown on a multi-size pattern. This
can be done by following the trend of
the lines and creating new ones. For
each size graded upward, measure
the distance from the previous line
and repeat the pattern, following the
angles at the corners.*

Shoulders: Adapting patterns for shoulder variations

It is essential that a garment fits well at the shoulders. Whether you have rounded, sloping, or square shoulders, there are different ways to improve the fit of a garment. By altering the position or angle of the shoulder seams, you can easily tailor the shape of the shoulder to suit your figure.

With the help of a friend and a mirror, take a look at the outline of your shoulders. They may be straight, sloping, or rounded, or perhaps uneven with one higher or lower than the other. Adding internal support using shoulder pads may be the best solution for improving the appearance of a tailored jacket or coat, but for pure comfort, changing the shoulder seam length, position, or angle is the best answer for an improved fit.

To assess the actual shape of your shoulders and whether they are close to standard, rounded, or sloping, place a line of pins through your shirt, along the center top of your shoulder. Take the front and back paper pattern pieces and pin them together along the shoulder seam,

pinching out the dart in the back shoulder if there is one. Place this over your shoulder and check whether the seam of the pattern lies directly over your line of pins. If not, measure the difference and make any adjustments to the pattern with this measurement. Turn the pattern over and check the second shoulder.

For rounded shoulders, cut and extend the back pattern and fold the front pattern up by the same amount, to remove the excess. This moves the shoulder seam forward to follow your natural shoulder position, which tilts to the front.

For sloping shoulders, alter the angle of the shoulder seam, sloping down from the neck, and then adjust the sleeve head to fit the new shape of the shoulder.

Before you start

Measure the length and compare this with the pattern shoulder measurement and make an assessment of whether your shoulders are square, standard, or sloping. Also, measure from your waist to the bone at the back of your neck and compare this with the paper pattern, too. Use the standard measurements listed in the pattern as a guide and also measure the pattern directly. This will give you an indication of how much of an adjustment needs to be made, if one must be made at all.

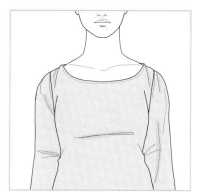

Sloping shoulders
If you have shoulders that slope downward and away from the neck, altering the angle of the shoulder seam will improve the fit and prevent folds of excess fabric from hanging over the shoulders. If you prefer to disguise this rather than adapt the pattern, make and fit shoulder pads to fill the gap between the body and the garment.

Square shoulders
If you have shoulders that are particularly angular and square, the hem of the garment will rise and the fabric around the shoulder area will pull and look awkward. By reshaping the angle of the shoulder seam and adapting the sleeve head to match, more space will be created for a comfortable fit.

Rounded shoulders
Rounded shoulders cause a jacket to pull across the back and often highlight a gaping neckline at the front. The jacket may also ride up at the back so that the hem does not sit level and hangs awkwardly (right). Moving the shoulder position will help to overcome these related problems and give a better, more comfortable fit (below, right).

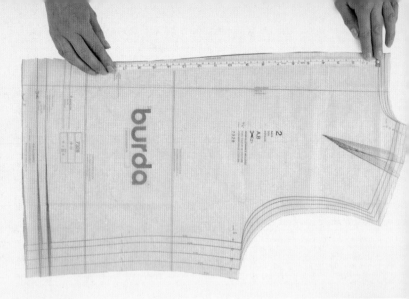

Adapting a pattern for rounded shoulders

This method shows how to move the shoulder seam forward, giving extra room for a rounded back and shoulders and removing any gaping wrinkles that tend to occur at the neckline.

Preparation: Collect the front and back bodice pattern piece.

1 Measure the back length on the pattern from waist to neck and compare this to your own back measurement. Get someone to measure you while you are standing in a comfortable position and not with your shoulders unnaturally straightened.

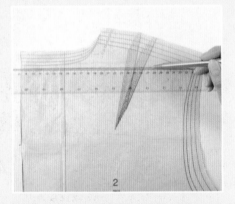

2 Using the back bodice pattern, mark a point 1 in (2.5 cm) below the center-back neck. Draw a line from here straight across the back to the upper part of the armhole.

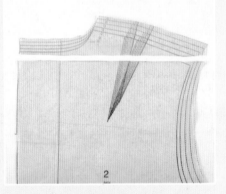

3 Cut along this line and move the pattern apart to the required amount to compensate for rounded shoulders. Keep the pieces parallel and level at the ends.

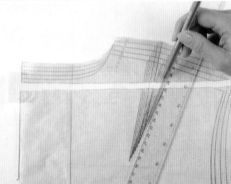

4 Tape the repositioned pattern pieces to a piece of paper. Reshape the shoulder dart if there is one. Measure and make a note of the amount added.

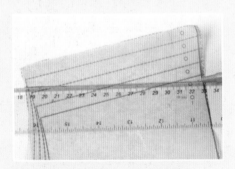

5 Take the front bodice piece and draw a line straight across the front shoulder, approximately 1 in (2.5 cm) from the outer shoulder point.

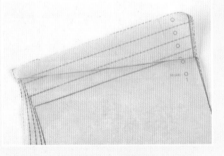

6 Make a tuck along the line on the front pattern piece equal to the amount added to the back shoulder and tape the fold in place.

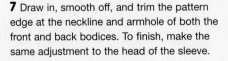

7 Draw in, smooth off, and trim the pattern edge at the neckline and armhole of both the front and back bodices. To finish, make the same adjustment to the head of the sleeve.

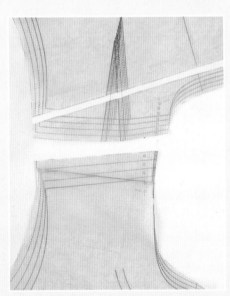

Adapting a pattern for sloping shoulders

By reshaping the angle of the shoulder seam, a dress, shirt, or jacket can be adjusted to achieve a better fit for someone with sloping shoulders.

Preparation: You will need the front, back, and sleeve pattern pieces.

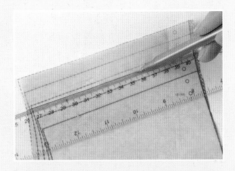

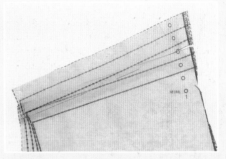

1 Draw the seam line onto the front shoulder of the bodice ⅝ in (1.5 cm) inside the cutting line. Cut along this line.

2 Pivoting at the neck edge, move the seam allowance down and over the shoulder point by approximately ½ in (1.3 cm), and tape it in place.

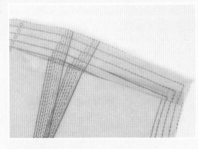

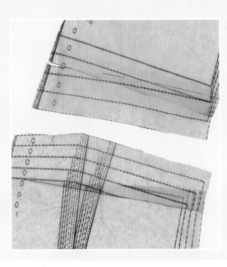

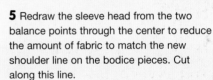

3 Repeat steps one and two with the back of the bodice.

4 Adjust the front and back shoulder pieces by the same amount.

5 Redraw the sleeve head from the two balance points through the center to reduce the amount of fabric to match the new shoulder line on the bodice pieces. Cut along this line.

Adapting patterns for square shoulders

For very square or angular shoulders, follow the instructions above, but move the pieces apart to lift the seam and create more room for the shoulders instead of moving the pattern pieces inward. Reshape the sleeve head to match the new shoulder line by adding height and extending the line outward.

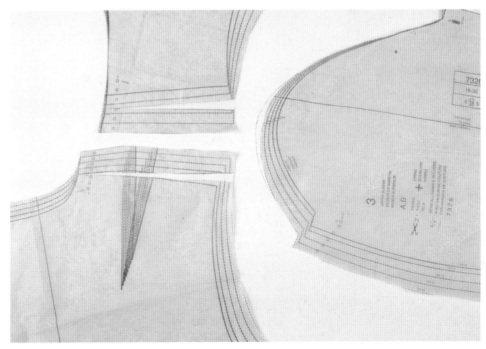

Shoulders: Shortening

If you have narrow shoulders and a jacket extends beyond your natural shoulder length, it will automatically make the whole garment seem too big. Shortening the sleeves or reducing the back width of the jacket will not help—recutting the shoulder pattern is the only answer.

Take your shoulder measurement accurately from the neck edge to the outer shoulder point. Compare this measurement with the standard measurements given on the pattern to confirm that you do have narrow shoulders compared to the standard sizing. The difference is the amount it is necessary to shorten the shoulder.

If standard measurements are not available for the shoulder length, measure the paper pattern across the shoulder (omitting the seam allowances) and compare this to your own shoulder length. This will indicate how much to reduce the shoulder length by. Be aware of the pattern style and that space may have been left to accommodate a shoulder pad.

Narrow shoulders
Garments can look oversized on those with narrow shoulders (left). To avoid clothes looking as though they are hanging off of the body, you will need to shorten the shoulder seam.

Additional considerations

Make sure you consider the seam allowance in the pattern (if there is one) and remember that the marked outer line is the cutting line and not the sewing line. Also, there may be a dart or additional ease allowed in the back shoulder to improve the garment fit.

Shortening the shoulder

This method shows how to reduce the length of the shoulder seam on a garment.

Preparation: You will need the pattern pieces for the front and back bodices.

1 Draw the seam line ⅝ in (1.5 cm) from the outside cutting line on the front shoulder. This is not necessary if the seam allowance is not included on the pattern.

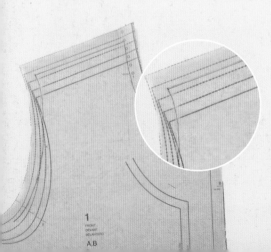

2 Measure the shoulder from the neck edge to shoulder point and compare this with the standard measurements of the pattern. Calculate how much to reduce the shoulder length by.

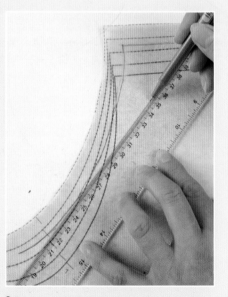

3 Draw a diagonal line with a ruler, from the midpoint of the shoulder seam line to the midpoint of the armhole on the stitching line. This forms a triangle shape.

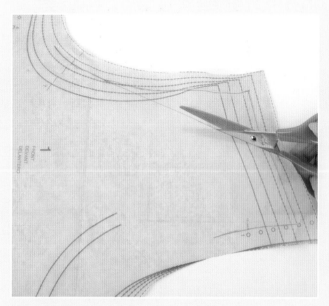

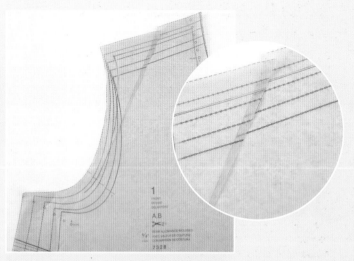

4 Cut along the line from the shoulder seam to the armhole, stopping just short of the edge. Do not cut through the armhole.

5 Mark a point on the pattern to show how much the shoulder length should be shortened by. Move the outer triangle inward to this point, pivoting at the armhole. Tape in place, with paper underneath.

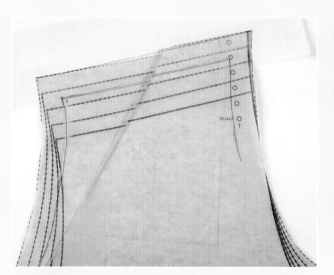

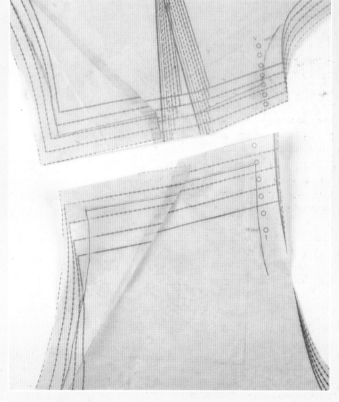

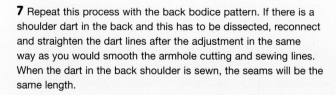

6 Redraw the new shoulder line with a ruler and smooth out the pivot point in the armhole.

7 Repeat this process with the back bodice pattern. If there is a shoulder dart in the back and this has to be dissected, reconnect and straighten the dart lines after the adjustment in the same way as you would smooth the armhole cutting and sewing lines. When the dart in the back shoulder is sewn, the seams will be the same length.

Lengthened shoulders

When the shoulder seams fit well, the finished top will be flattering.

Shoulders: Lengthening

If you have broader-than-average shoulders, you will tend to find that clothes do not fit well across the shoulders and may appear small on you, although the rest of the garment fits well. Extending the shoulder seam of the bodice pattern of a jacket, coat, blouse, or dress is a simple task. The entire garment will look and feel much better as a result.

This alteration requires cutting diagonally through the shoulder to the armhole, allowing the shoulder seam to be opened up. This extension is held in place with paper and tape to permanently adapt the pattern for your own perfect, personal fit. Extend both the front and back shoulder pattern pieces so that they will be the same length when sewing up the garment. If there is additional ease or a dart included in the back shoulder, this will make no difference as the amount of ease or the dart will take up any excess room and the seams will still fit when sewn. You will need to add the same amount to the back as you do to the front and redraw the dart if it is affected by the alteration.

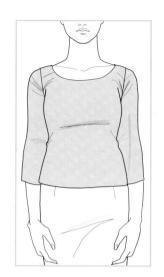

Broad shoulders

If the shoulder seam is too short it will be uncomfortable to wear and will look as if the dress or jacket is too small, with pulling across the shoulder and possibly the neckline too (left).
To improve the fit and look of a garment for those with broad shoulders it is necessary to lengthen the shoulder seam.

Before you start

Get a friend to accurately measure your shoulder length and compare it with the standard measurements of the pattern to establish whether your shoulder bones are longer than average and that the alteration is necessary. Measure from the crease, where your neck meets your shoulder, to the outer point of your shoulder bone.

Lengthening the shoulder

This method shows how to add length to the shoulder seam on any bodice pattern, whether it is a jacket or a dress.

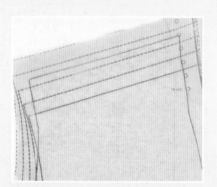

1 Unless the pattern you are using has no seam allowances included, draw the seam line ⅝ in (1.5 cm) inside and parallel to the cutting line.

2 Measure the shoulder from neck edge to shoulder point and compare this with the standard measurements of the pattern. Calculate how much to add to the shoulder length.

3 Draw a diagonal line with a ruler from the midpoint of the shoulder seam line to the midpoint of the armhole on the stitching line. This forms a triangle shape.

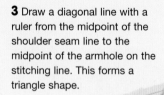

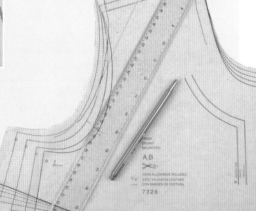

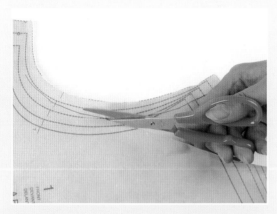

4 Cut along the line from the shoulder seam to the armhole, stopping just short of the edge. Do not cut through the armhole edge.

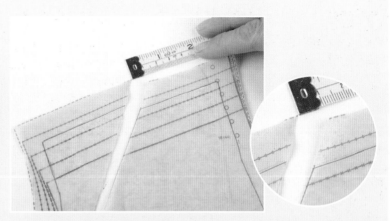

5 Move the outer triangle outward, pivoting at the armhole, until the correct length is achieved on the shoulder seam.

6 Place a piece of paper underneath the pattern and shoulder seam and hold it in position with sticky tape.

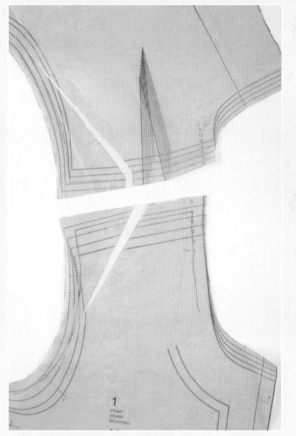

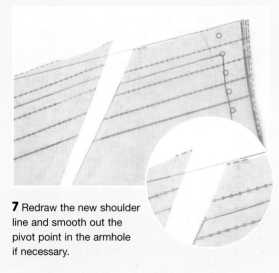

7 Redraw the new shoulder line and smooth out the pivot point in the armhole if necessary.

8 Repeat this process with the back bodice pattern. When the back shoulder dart is sewn, the two seams will be the same length.

Neckline: Too loose

It is important that a neckline sits comfortably over the collarbone whether it is a round, "V," or fancy-shaped neckline, or one with a collar attached. The neck edge should be symmetrical and lie flat on the neck and chest. This is a part of the body that can highlight a poor fit and it is essential that any extra fabric is removed for a smooth finish.

The first step is to establish how much fabric needs to be removed from the neckline. This can be done using the paper pattern placed over the body. With the paper pattern in place, just pinch out the extra pattern to make a flat edge. This is explained fully in "Before you start" on the opposite page.

There are two ways to deal with a gaping neckline and remove the excess material. One is simple and requires very little work, while the other involves more manipulation of the pattern before the fabric is cut out. Both result in a smoother finish.

You can either redraw the center-front line of the bodice pattern, taking fabric out of the front neck (but not the hem) or you can cut into the neck edge from the bust point and open up the bodice seam or dart. If the bodice has no seams, the first method is the one to choose. For a well-fitting, shaped bodice, the second method allows the extra fabric to be dispersed into the seam or dart without being noticed.

Adapting a gaping neckline

These two methods show how to get rid of excess fabric at a neckline by altering the bodice pattern pieces. The option on the opposite page is a simple method for reducing fullness, while the method below requires more pattern manipulation.

Method 1

Use the bust as a pivot point.

Preparation: You will need the front bodice pattern piece.

1 Find the position of the bust point 1½ in (4 cm) beyond the point of the dart and draw a line from the bust point to the middle of the neckline.

2 Cut through the center of the dart to the bust point. Note: The dart may lie on the waist or side seam, or the bodice may have a princess seam, in which case the seam is opened up slightly more and will not be noticed when the seam is sewn.

3 Make a fold along the line from the bust point to the neckline, removing approximately ¼ in (6 mm) of fabric. This opens up the dart.

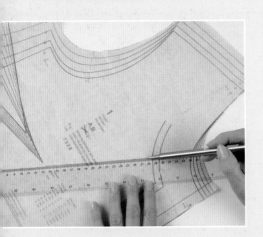
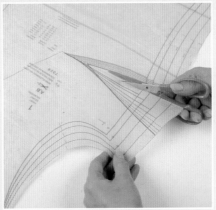
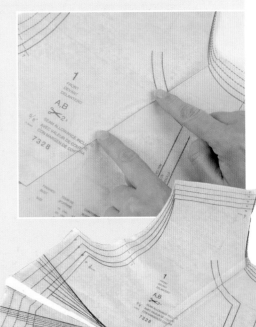

4 Place paper below the dart and tape the manipulated pattern in place. Redraw the dart, finding the dart point 1½ in (4 cm) short of the bust point. The fullness is now removed from the neckline.

Before you start

Pin the bodice paper pattern over your clothes, securing it to the shoulder, side seam, and center front. Pin away any excess paper at the neck to get rid of the gaping that would appear on a finished garment. Unfold and measure the tuck to see how much you will need to remove at the neck edge.

Gaping neckline

Excess fullness at the neck looks untidy, and on a low neckline it may reveal more than you wish. The gaping may be caused by rounded shoulders or a hollow chest, but the methods on these pages and on pages 65–67 will correct the problem.

Method 2

Adjust the pattern at the center front.

Preparation: You will need the front bodice pattern piece.

1 Mark a point at the seam line at the neckline approximately ¼ in (6 mm) in from the center-front fold, adjusting the exact measurement as necessary.

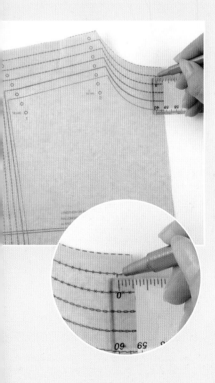

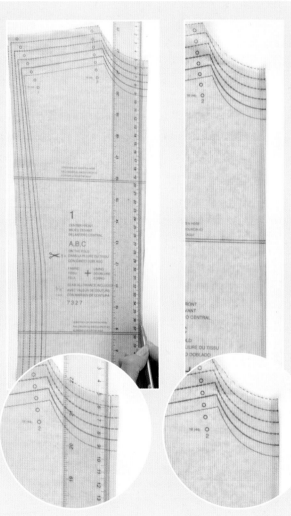

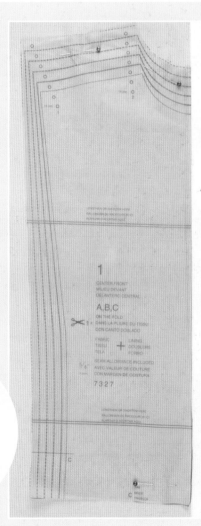

2 Draw a line from the neck to the point at the center front on the waist or hem. Use this as the new center-front line.

3 Fold back the center front along the line or cut it away.

4 Place the new center front on the folded fabric. If the center front is against a seam, the fullness removed is lost in the seam.

Neckline: Too high and tight

It is important that a neckline lies comfortably around the neck and that it is not too tight or restrictive. Any pulling or tightness around the neck must be dealt with and removed for a garment to look and feel good.

In most cases, dropping the neckline at the front and the back or the shoulder will help.

If adapting the pattern to create more room around the neck fails to give a comfortable fit, then the answer is to adjust the neck at the toile stage (see page 136).

A tight neck may be a result of the neck length or circumference or even the angle of the shoulders. If there is creasing around the neck, a shoulder adjustment may be the most appropriate alteration.

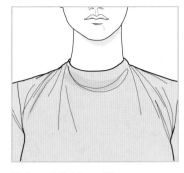

High and tight neckline
An ill-fitting neckline can look and feel uncomfortable (above). Reshaping the neckline will eliminate this issue.

Dropping or opening up the neckline

If a neckline is very high and restrictive, it will be necessary to reshape it for a more comfortable fit. For other neckline reshaping options, see page 65–66.

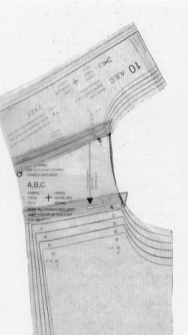

Preparation: You will need the front bodice and back pattern pieces. It may be the case—as in this example—that there is a yoke instead of a shoulder seam, but this makes no difference to the method of alteration.

1 Pin the neckline pattern pieces together at the shoulder seam or yoke panel. This will give half a neckline from center front to center back.

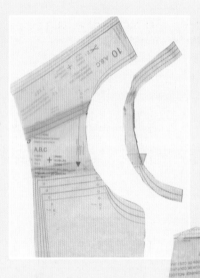

2 Cut away the seam allowance from the neckline.

3 Draw the new neckline; lowering at the center front, widening at the shoulders, and dropping very slightly at the back. Make sure a smooth and natural line is created.

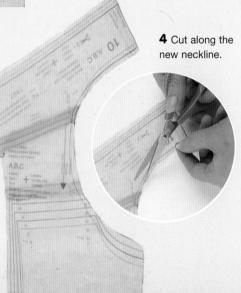

4 Cut along the new neckline.

5 Unpin the pattern pieces and add a seam allowance of ⅝ in (1.5 cm) to each adapted piece by taping paper beneath each pattern piece.

Neckline: Altering the shape

It is important that a neckline is an appropriate shape that flatters the face and figure.

Changing the neckline shape

Prepare the pattern pieces as explained for adapting a tight neckline by pinning the front and back together (see page 64). Remember, this may include a yoke too, as in our example. Fold along the seam lines and join with pins, then redraw the new neckline shaping on the seam line. Place the pinned pattern piece over your shoulder to check that the level and shape are appropriate. Add a ⅝ in (1.5 cm) seam allowance to all the pattern pieces.

Options for neckline shapes

It is essential that a neckline flatters the figure, and as you can see here, it is easy to adapt or completely change the neckline shape on a garment. Choose a pattern you like and make style changes to the neckline as necessary.

To alter the neckline shape of a bodice, pin the pattern pieces together at the neckline, then redraw the shape you would prefer.

Adapting neckline shape

You may wish to change the outline of a neck edge for fashion reasons, adapting it and creating a more flattering shape.

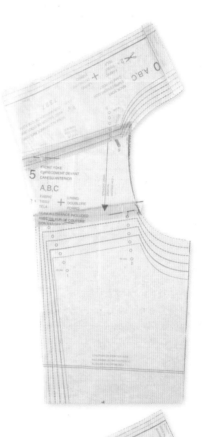

Crew

A crew neck is flattering on most women, providing it is not cut too high and tight to the neck. Smaller-busted women may prefer to avoid a crew neck, since it can emphasize a small bust.

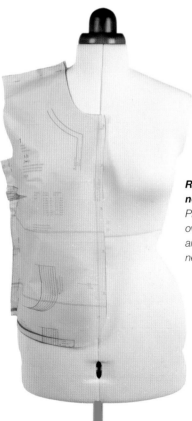

Reworking a neckline

Pin pattern pieces over a dress form and reshape the neckline as required.

Scoop

A scoop shape is flattering to most women and works particularly well on those with narrow shoulders, but steer clear of a very low cut, except for evening wear.

Square

This works well on women with narrow shoulders but can reveal too much skin. Choose a plain square or one with a bold border to add interest.

Sweetheart

This pretty neckline suits those with a large bust, but it can reveal too much if the shape is cut low. Add piping or lace to frame the shape for a special finish.

"V"

A "V"-neckline suits most women because it creates a long and elegant neck. It is a good opportunity to show off a pretty necklace or scarf, too.

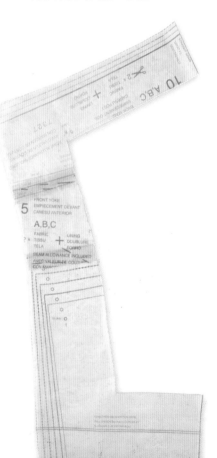

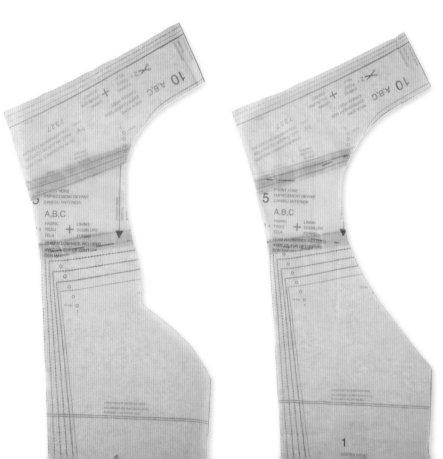

Faced neckline

A facing is a good option for most neckline shapes. It is easy to do and facilitates a neat finish—essential in such a prominent part of a garment. The neckline area is normally interfaced to keep it from losing its shape.

Preparation: Sew the shoulder seams and finish the edges.

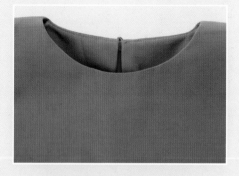

Front
Back

1 Cut out the facing pattern in fabric and in interfacing material. Note: If a pattern is not provided for a facing, make one following the shape of the neckline and approximately 2½ in (6 cm) deep.

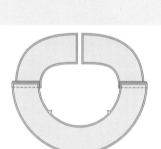

2 Fuse the interfacing to the wrong side of the neck facing. Then, sew the pieces together. Finish the outer edge.

3 Place the facing for the neckline with right sides together, matching seams and all pattern markings. Pin and sew together, reinforcing any stress points, such as a "V" point, with an extra row of stitching.

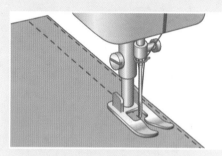

4 To finish, understitch the seam allowance to the facing, or topstitch and edge stitch (if necessary) with either a matching or contrasting thread, depending on the required look.

Neck band

On a T-shirt or casual top, the neckline is sometimes finished with a folded band. This is especially popular with stretch fabrics, making the shirt comfortable to wear and easy to slip on and off over the head.

Preparation: Complete shoulder seams.

1 Cut the neck band to size. This will be double the finished width with seam allowance added and approximately one-fifth (20 percent) less than the required length. It will stretch as it is sewn and support the neckline when completed.

2 With right sides together, sew the neck band into a circle and fold in half lengthwise (with wrong sides on the inside).

3 Mark the neck band and neckline into equal quarters and pin together with all the raw edges even. Sew the layers together, stretching the band to fit the neckline in the process.

Neckline: Collars

A collar adds a frame to a neckline, and there are many designs to choose from. Seasonal fashion influences the popular collars of the moment and dictates the size and shape. Careful choice of collar type gives balance to a garment and will flatter your figure, emphasizing the neck and shoulders.

Designing collar patterns

A plain garment becomes your own unique design when you create a pattern for the collar. You can choose to individualize a standard outfit with these little touches. Follow the basic instructions for making a shirt collar and be adventurous with the collar point, rounding it off or elongating it to suit your own style. Alternatively, you can design a collar to lay flat over the shoulders.

Shirt collar

A traditional shirt collar is constructed in two parts, although a single shaped piece is often used for less formal shirts.

Preparation: (for a one-piece shirt collar) Collect the yoke and front of the shirt, or the front and back pieces if the style has a shoulder seam. You will need to work from these so that the collar fits the shirt.

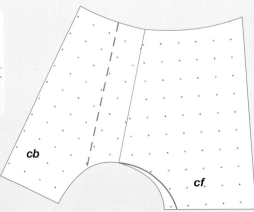

1 Remove the seam allowance from the neckline, if there is one, and lower the front neckline by ⅝ in (1.5 cm). Reshape in a natural curve.

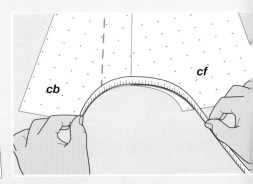

2 Measure the neckline from center front to center back.

3 To make the collar pattern:

a Draw a rectangle 4 in (10 cm) deep by half of the neckline measurement above. Mark the lower left corner as "6."
b Divide the neckline measurement by four and mark a quarter point from the right side. Call this "1."
c Draw a horizontal line through the rectangle 1⅝ in (4 cm) above the base. Mark the left end of the line "5."
d On this line, mark a point ¼ in (6 mm) to the left of the right edge of the rectangle and call this "4."
e Mark a point ¼ in (6 mm) above the bottom right corner. Call this "2."
f Draw a line from the quarter point "1" to "2" and extend this by ⅝ in (1.5 cm) to point "3." Finish the collar stand by joining up points "3" and "4". Draw in the shape of the collar fall with a point or curve as appropriate for the design.

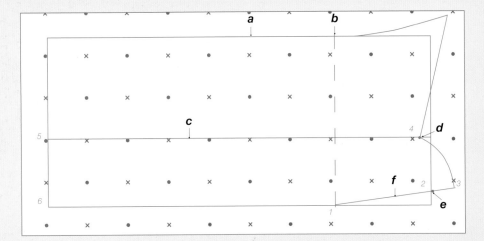

4 Treat the collar as one piece and add seam allowances to the outer edges.

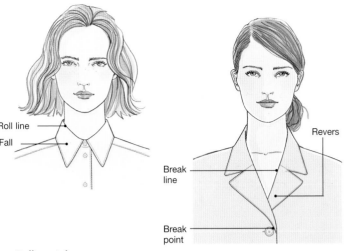

Roll line
Fall

Revers
Break line
Break point

Collar styles

Collars may lie flat around the neckline and sit over the shoulders, or stand up at the neck. Jackets and coats have "revers," which are an extension of the facing and lie back on the chest. Where the revers fold back, this is the "break point" and the edge is referred to as the "break line." A traditional shirt collar has a "stand" (the upright part next to the neck) and "fall" (the visible part that lies over the top). The "roll line" is the edge where the stand and fall meet.

Top collars and under collars

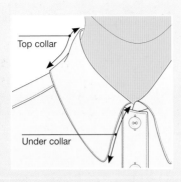

Top collar

Under collar

When constructing collar patterns, it is important to remember that all collars have a top collar and an under collar, or facing. This finishes the collar edge and eliminates bulk. The top collar has farther to travel from the neckline to the collar edge.

The under collar has a shorter distance to travel. The amount by which the under collar should be shorter is dependent on the thickness of the fabric. Start with $\frac{1}{8}$ in (3 mm) shorter and try the collar out. To make the under collar, shorten the depth by $\frac{1}{8}$ in (3 mm) at the center-back neck, continue with the $\frac{1}{8}$ in (3mm) past the shoulder notch, and gently blend into the center-front neck edge.

Peter Pan collar

A Peter Pan collar is an example of a flat collar that lies on the chest and shoulders rather than at the neck with a stand, like a shirt collar. The pattern of a flat collar is drafted using the bodice pattern pieces. The shape and size is determined by the style choice and a well-fitting bodice.

Preparation: Cut out the front and back pattern pieces of the bodice and include the yoke if there is one.

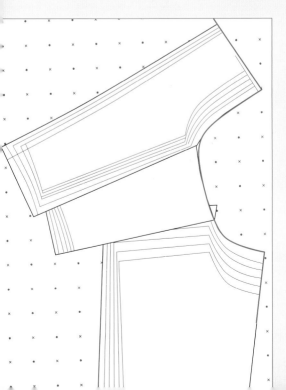

1 Pin the pattern pieces that form the neckline of the dress or blouse together.

2 Place pattern paper under the neckline and trace the neckline from center front to center back. Note: If your pattern includes a seam allowance remove this by cutting away $\frac{5}{8}$ in (1.5 cm).

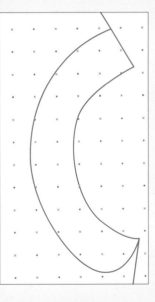

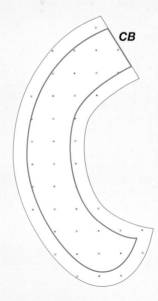

CB

3 Draw the outline of the collar in the shape and size that you want and round off the front edge.

4 Add seam allowances to the Peter Pan collar and it is ready to use.

Bust: Raising or lowering

Getting the bust level right when fitting clothes is vital for both comfort and fit. With a few simple adjustments to the length, it is an easy task to raise or lower the bust position in a pattern to create a perfect fit.

The first step is to identify how your bust compares with the standard pattern. From there it can be raised or lowered accordingly. Wearing your best-fitting bra, lightly tie a length of soft elastic around the bust at the widest part (at the nipple level). Measure from your mid-shoulder to the bust level and take a note of this measurement. Now, measure the pattern from the middle of the shoulder to the bust line. If your measurement is larger than the pattern, you have a low bust, and if it is a smaller measurement, you have a high bust. All you need to do now is adjust the pattern to reflect your figure.

Raising or lowering the bust level in a pattern to improve the fit is simple, whether the garment is constructed with seams or darts. The pattern is marked horizontally above and below the bust position and either lifted or lowered by cutting and folding the pattern as required. When the adjustment has been made, the pattern edges—where the tissue has been cut and moved apart or folded into a tuck—are smoothed off to give a natural line. You will finish with a perfectly fitting bodice.

Take time to adapt a pattern for a great-fitting bodice.

High bust

If the bust level of a garment is too low for a model, the bodice will be tight above the bust line and there will be excess fabric sitting below (above). This will look and feel uncomfortable to wear. By altering the pattern, a smooth finish will be achieved.

Adapting a pattern to raise bust level (in a princess-seam style)

If your body is relatively short between the shoulder and bust, you have a high bust and may find that your bra straps need to be tightened to get a comfortable fit. Adjusting bra straps is easy enough, but for a dress or top, a more permanent adjustment is required.

Preparation: Select the front bodice pattern piece or pieces for your garment as well as the back. Calculate the amount you need to raise the bust level of the pattern by comparing your measurement with the pattern.

1 Patterns will vary and may have darts or princess seams to give shaping for the bust. Draw one horizontal line across the chest of the bodice pattern just above the bust level and a second line parallel to the first and below the bust line.

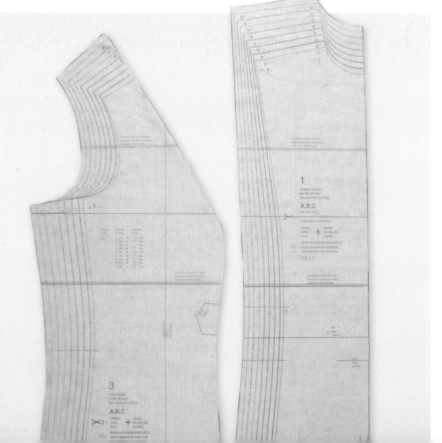

2 Make a tuck along the upper line and remove the excess length from the shoulder to the bust level. This amount will be the pattern measurement minus the actual body measurement from shoulder to bust line. If there are two or more pattern pieces, make the fold at the same level on all parts.

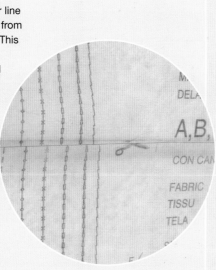

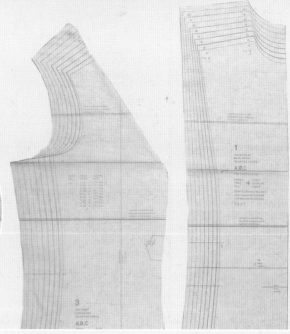

3 Cut through the lower line below the bust in all the pattern pieces.

4 Move the pattern pieces apart, where you have cut them, by the same measurement that the upper line was reduced. Place paper below and tape the manipulated pattern in position to hold it. This will ensure that the bodice measurement remains the same even though the bust level has been raised.

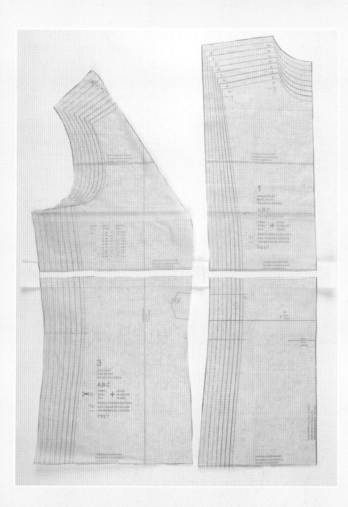

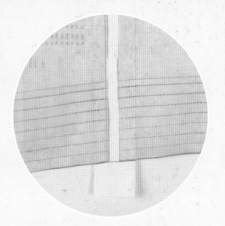

5 Smooth out the sides for a natural line.

Note: To lower the bust in a princess-seam style, cut along the upper line and fold the lower line.

Adapting a pattern to lower bust level (in a style with bust darts)

If your body is relatively long between the shoulder and bust, you have a low bust and may find that you need to adjust your patterns to get a good fit. Lowering the bust level involves the opposite of the instructions given previously. This time we will demonstrate the alteration in a bodice with a bust dart to show an alternative. Raising or lowering the bust level is easy in all styles.

Preparation: Select the front bodice pattern piece for your garment. Calculate the amount you need to lower the bust level of the pattern by comparing your measurement with the pattern.

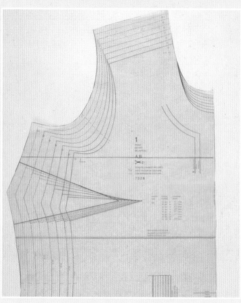

1 Draw one horizontal line across the chest of the bodice pattern just above the bust dart and a second line parallel to the first and below the dart.

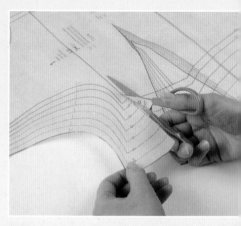

2 Cut the pattern apart along the upper line.

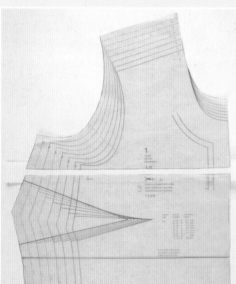

3 Move the pattern pieces apart to add length from the shoulder to the bust level. This amount will be your actual body measurement minus the pattern measurement from shoulder to bust line. Place paper below the pattern and tape in place to secure the new position.

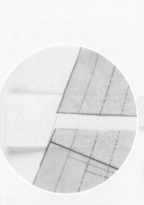

4 Smooth off the cutting lines to give a natural join where the pattern has been adjusted.

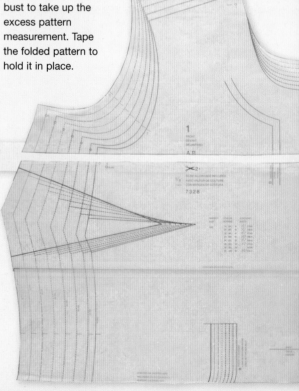

5 Make a fold along the line below the bust to take up the excess pattern measurement. Tape the folded pattern to hold it in place.

Bust: Darts

Darts are an excellent way of introducing shape so that we can make clothes to fit our rounded bodies. They are especially useful for accommodating the bust and can be placed in a variety of positions to give the silhouette we require.

Any standard pattern with a dart or darts can be adapted if you would prefer to have them in a different position. Generally, they are placed horizontally from the side seam to the bust point, but they can be angled from the side seam or run from the shoulder or waist to give the fit and the style desired. Moving a dart can make an entire outfit more flattering, so consider repositioning darts to improve the look you want. Simple optical illusions can occur according to the positioning and angle of seams or darts on a garment. For example, a vertical bodice dart from bust point to shoulder may draw the eye up and down, increasing height. A horizontal dart from the bust point to side seam may pull the eye sideways, creating an impression of added width/breadth in a figure.

   To change a dart position, cut into the bodice from the outside edge of the pattern to the bust point and open up a new dart along this cut. As you open up the new dart, the old dart is folded out and the fullness is removed. As a result, the bodice still fits the same body shape but the excess fabric is removed from a different place on the pattern. This type of pattern adaptation is very logical and easy to carry out, giving rise to many style alternatives and opportunities for the creative designer. It allows the use of single or multiple darts or even the chance to create seams from adjoining darts (as in a princess seam).

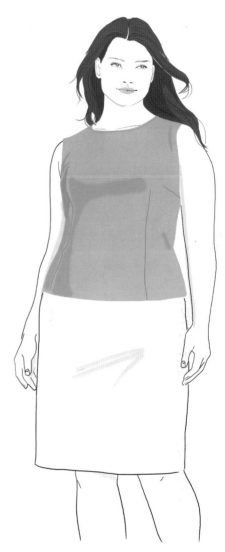

Shaping using darts
Bust and waist darts shape the bodice for a good fit.

Dart possibilities
Darts can be placed anywhere around the bust point.

Dart manipulation

Darts are easy to move by cutting, folding, and repositioning where you need them; just follow the instructions and see how easy it is.

Preparation: Cut out the front bodice pattern piece in the size you require.

1 Trace off the bodice pattern onto pattern paper and mark the bust dart(s) in their existing position or positions.

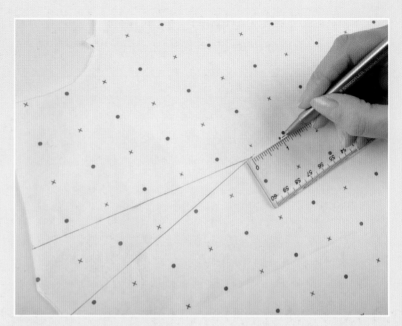

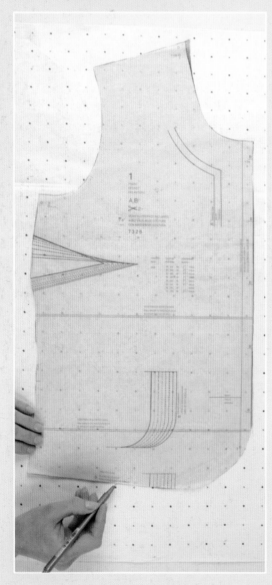

2 Find the bust point, which is beyond the point of the bust dart. For a good fit, the dart always stops short of the widest part of the bust.

3 Draw a line from the bust point to the new dart position.

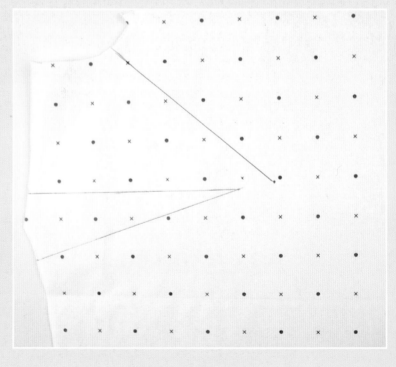

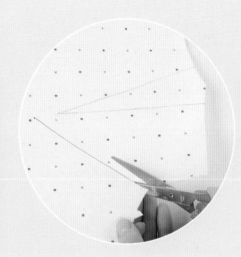

4 Cut along the new dart line to the bust point and open up the new dart. At the same time, close up the old dart with a fold.

5 Place paper below the new dart and tape it open. Mark the end point of the dart (the same distance short of the bust point as the previous dart) and draw the new dart in place. Smooth off all edges.

Bust: Altering bodice with darts

Darts are used to provide shaping in a bodice. These can be positioned at any angle radiating from the widest part—the bust point. By simple manipulation, darts can be moved to the most appropriate position for the figure and style. More importantly, they can be adjusted to accommodate the bust, too. Since most patterns are drafted for standard sizes with a "B" cup (defined as a 2-in/5-cm difference between chest and bust measurements), more room has to be created for a larger cup size. As with all adjustments for a large bust, select the pattern size for the general frame based on back width, shoulder length, and chest measurement rather than choosing a size to fit the bust, as this will be too large.

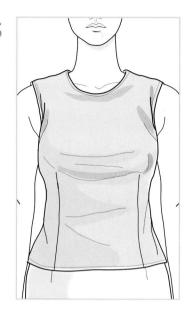

Cup size too large for bodice
If the wearer has a large cup measurement for the bodice size of a garment, the fabric will be pulled or stretched across the bust causing wrinkling above and below, as seen here. This may even pull the side seams forward and create excess fabric around the neckline.

Before you start

Measure the body and compare these measurements with the standard sizes printed in the pattern. A large cup size will be obvious as it will appear as an anomaly compared to the other measurements. Cut out the pattern for the most appropriate size, ignoring the bust.

A bodice may have one or two pairs of darts to give the shaping required. These may be from the waist, the side seam, the armhole, or even the shoulder. Two pairs of darts make it easier to adapt a pattern for a larger cup size, as smaller amounts of fabric can be spread over more areas rather than a large amount of cloth being added to just one pair of darts. As a large bust alteration requires extra fabric to run both lengthwise and widthwise, two pairs make this process easier.

Check that the bust position is at the correct level (see page 70) and make any necessary adjustment to account for this before making the dart alterations. Having selected the correct size and prepared the pattern front, the paper is cut and the pieces moved apart. When the correct adjustment has been achieved (with room for the bust and "ease" for wear) darts and pattern edges will be redrawn. Make up a toile to check the fit before continuing.

Enlarging the bust of a bodice with darts
In this example, a size 18 pattern was used.

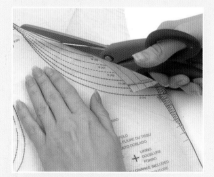

1 Cut out all the pattern pieces in the appropriate size and select the bodice front.

2 Draw a line from the point of the waist dart to the center front (horizontal to the hem and perpendicular to the front edge) and join the dart points.

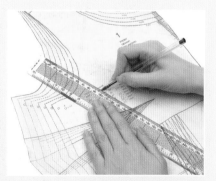

3 Draw a line from the bust dart point to the armhole. On a pattern where the dart sits in the armhole rather than the side seam, draw the line from the bust dart point to the side seam.

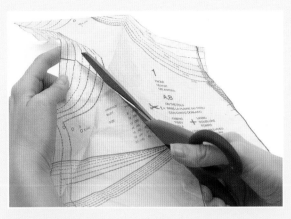

4 Cut along the lines and through the middle of the darts.

5 Measure the body from mid-shoulder to waist through the bust point. Compare this measurement with the center-front pattern piece. With a strip of paper placed below the cut, move the pattern pieces apart the corresponding amount and tape in place. This extends the length to accommodate the larger cup size.

6 Measure the body from the side to the center front—horizontally through the bust at the widest part. Add the required amount of ease (see pages 46–47 for how to calculate this) to this measurement.

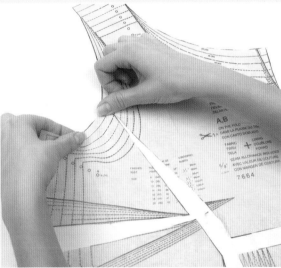

7 Pivot the underarm pattern piece at the armhole (moving it out and up) and move the lower side pattern piece down and out correspondingly, making sure to keep it level with the hem of the center front. Check that the pattern movement is sufficient and readjust if necessary.

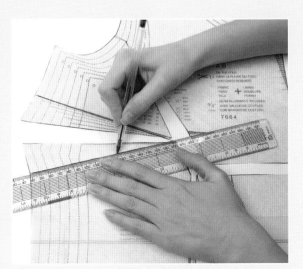

8 When the pattern pieces are in the correct position, tape to the paper placed underneath. Redraw the darts (which will now be wider to match the shaping of the body) and the edges of the pattern to form smooth joins where they meet.

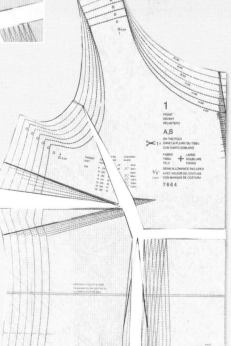

Bust: Altering a princess seam

A princess-seam dress or top has vertical seams in the front that run from the hem and through the bust, either to the shoulder or the armhole. The position of these seams makes it easy to adapt the fit by removing fabric for a smaller bust and providing more fabric and shaping for a larger bust.

Take accurate measurements

The most important step is to measure accurately, as this will allow the selection of the most appropriate size. Locate the size chart that accompanies your pattern, giving full measurement details (these will either be printed on the outside of the envelope or inside on the instruction sheet or pattern tissue). Compare your measurements with the chart and circle the relevant numbers on the printed chart. If a large bust is the problem, then this will appear as an anomaly. To select the size to cut out, ignore the bust size and choose the size that best matches your other measurements.

Assuming that the pattern made up in this size will fit except for the bust, the next step is to create more room for the bust. By cutting and moving the pattern pieces apart and following the instructions below, it is easy to create the space required for a large bust.

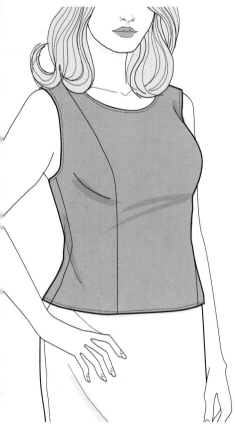

Using princess seams
Adjust princess seams for a perfect bodice fit.

Ill-fitting bodice
Where the bust is too large for the garment, as well as appearing too tight across the front, the vertical side seams will pull forward and the horizontal waist seam will rise up (above). After pattern adjustments for a large bust, the seams sit in their correct positions with no pulling or gaping across the bust, at the armhole, or at the neckline.

Enlarging the bust of a garment with princess seams

In this example, a size 18 pattern was used.

1 Find the bust point on the paper pattern. If this is not marked it will be at the widest part. Mark the positions on the side front.

2 Draw a line parallel to the hem on the center front and cut along this line.

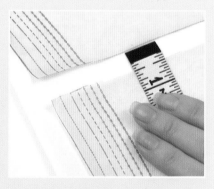

3 Measure the body from shoulder to bust point to waist. Compare this with the measurement on the center front pattern piece and move the pieces accordingly.

4 Tape the pattern to paper placed below to secure it.

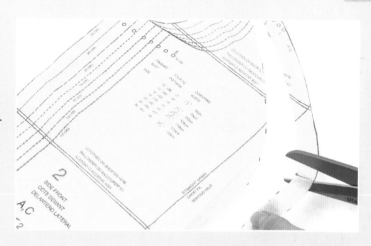

5 Cut into the seam allowance at the bust point and from there along the seam allowance to the armhole and hem.

6 Pivot the two seam allowance pieces at the armhole and hem, moving them apart at the bust point. Move these pieces the same amount as the center-front pieces.

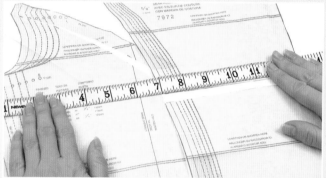

7 Measure the body from the side to the center front horizontally through the bust line. Add the required amount of ease (see pages 46–47 for calculating this) to this measurement and check this against the adjusted pattern pieces (overlap them at the seam allowance when measuring).

The finished pieces can be used to create your perfectly fitted garment.

8 Smooth out the seams and edges.

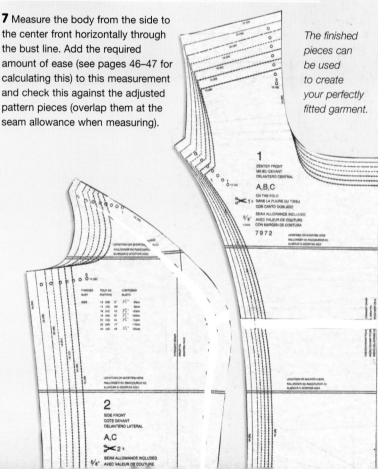

Bust: Altering a high-waist style or empire line

A dress or top with a high waist can be very flattering for some figures. It can give the illusion of changing body proportion by increasing leg length for those with a relatively longer back and shorter legs or for pear-shaped silhouettes (see page 22). We have seen how getting a good fit around the bust line in patterns with darts and vertical seams is possible, but high-waisted styles have a horizontal seam directly below the bust and this gives yet another possibility to create an improved fit. In a style where there is a close-fitting bodice with a seam just below the bust, the darts often run from the horizontal seam at the base of the bodice panel to the bust points.

High-waisted dress
A well-fitting high-waisted style can be very flattering.

Adapting an empire style

If you have a cup size larger than a "B," most styles will be too small across the bust. Here, we show how to enlarge the bodice panel in a high-waisted dress for an improved fit. Choose the pattern size most appropriate for a good fit around the rib cage and not one to match the bust measurement. These instructions explain how to increase the bodice panel for a larger cup.

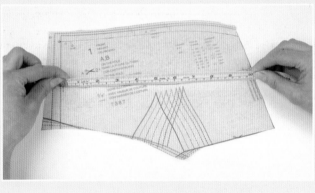

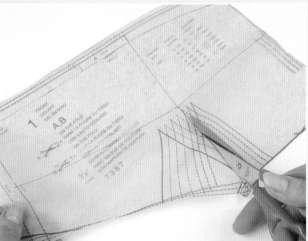

Preparation: Separate the bodice front pattern piece from the other pattern pieces and cut it out in your size. Have the bodice back piece at hand.

1 Measure the following parts on the pattern and compare these with your own body measurements divided by two:
• Across the top edge of the bodice panel (center front to side seam, not including the side seam allowance).
• Across the bust at bust level (the widest part, but not including the side seam allowance).

2 Draw through the bust point on the pattern with two straight lines—one horizontal and one vertical. Cut along these lines to separate the bodice into four parts.

As long as the measurement around the rib cage, just below the bust, fits well, then all the necessary changes can be made to the bodice parts. For a larger cup size, extra fabric can be added to this panel. For a smaller bust, the panel can be reduced in size to fit. Manipulating the darts in the bodice panel allows us to create a new bust size that will still fit the horizontal seam of the lower dress.

Since most commercial patterns are drafted with a standard bust measurement of a "B" cup, most women will need to alter their pattern to improve the fit. Whether enlarging or reducing the bodice to suit the cup size is required, this cannot be done purely by taking in or letting out the side seams. The darts must be altered to give more room to accommodate a larger cup size or to remove fabric from the bodice for a smaller cup. After adjusting the dart size and outline, further reshaping may be required for the front bodice panel to continue to fit the pieces around it. Remember, if you are altering the fit to accommodate a larger cup size, more fabric is needed in the bodice panel to increase the coverage; conversely, a smaller cup requires less fabric.

Bodice too tight

When the cup size is "C" or larger, the bodice pulls across the bust and it is tight across the chest and under the arm. Enlarging the bodice panel allows a better fit around the body. It also covers more of the bust, sitting at a higher level on the chest.

Bodice too loose

An "A" or "AA" cup will leave the bodice loose and unfilled, showing excess material in the bodice panel. Making pattern alterations to reduce the fabric in the bodice gives an attractive, smooth finish across the bust.

3 Move the pattern pieces apart, sideways to match the body measurements (through and over the bust) and pivot horizontally from the side seam by ¼ in (6 mm) per cup size. This increases the amount of fabric in both directions to cover the larger cup. Stick the newly positioned pattern pieces onto paper.

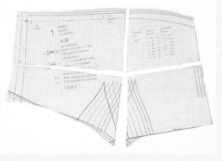

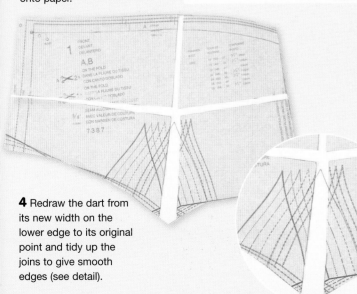

4 Redraw the dart from its new width on the lower edge to its original point and tidy up the joins to give smooth edges (see detail).

Reducing the bodice for a small bust

Note: To reduce the size of the pattern for a smaller bust, cut the pattern in the same way and slide the pattern pieces inward to decrease the size. Tape in place, redraw the dart, and reshape the pattern edges. As there will be less fabric in the bodice, the finished dress will provide a better fit and there will be no excess fabric across the front of this panel.

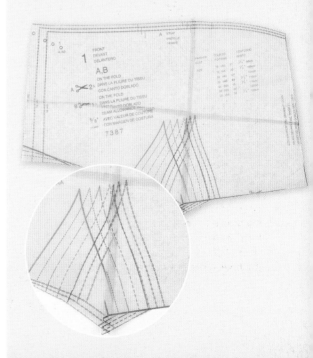

Adding darts
Even the fit of a bodice without any shaping can be improved by including darts.

Bust: Alterations in a bodice without darts

Garments normally have seams and darts to provide shaping. Some clothes, for example those made from stretch fabric, like T-shirts, do not always need them. If you need to enlarge the bust of a dartless and seamless bodice, there are two ways to approach it. One is to add width to the side seams, and the second is to open up the bodice to create darts. Both methods provide more room to follow the contours of the body and do not rely only on the flexibility of stretchy fabric to provide a good fit.

In order for an unshaped bodice to go around the body, it generally has to be larger so the extra fullness remains where a dart or seam would otherwise remove it and improve the fit. This works on a slim catwalk model, but for more curvy figures this only results in adding the illusion of width and weight to the body. Wearing large and shapeless garments gives some women the belief that they are concealing their size under the fabric; however, they actually look much slimmer when wearing closer-fitting or tailored garments.

Adding width by altering seams
The simplest way to increase the size of a top without darts or seams is to extend the side seams of the front.

Preparation: Measure from side to side across the fullest part of your bust, keeping the tape measure level. Divide this figure by two to give the measurement from the center front to the side seam. Cut out the front and sleeve pattern pieces in the appropriate size, according to your frame and not your bust measurement.

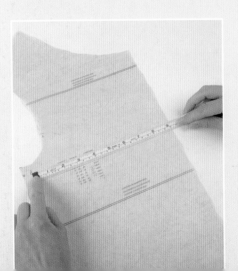

1 Measure from the side seam line across the bust to the center front of the pattern, and compare this with the body measurement. Subtract the pattern measurement from the body measurement to give the amount that has to be added to the side seam.

2 Tape paper below the pattern and add the amount required to the side seam.

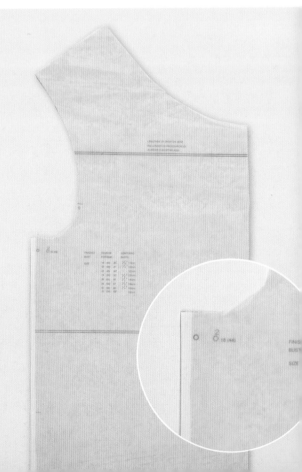

A small or a large amount of shaping can be added to a plain top or dress, depending on what is required. A simple bust dart from the underarm may be all that is necessary to improve the appearance of a garment that would otherwise look shapeless. For a more sophisticated fit, a bust and waist dart will give more shape and dispose of a larger amount of surplus material.

Here are two ways to help achieve a better shape from a pattern that does not have seams or darts:

Adding width

By adding a small amount to the side seams, there will be additional fabric to cover the bust around the body. Assuming the back fits well, no alteration is required to this section. The drawback of this method is that there is extra fabric around the waist and tummy, as there are no darts or seams to improve the shape. In a similar way, you can reduce the width of a garment for a small bust by reducing the width of the front side seams.

Adding darts

If you are not using stretch fabric and you need to add some shaping to a bodice to accommodate a larger bust, you can insert darts to provide more shape. This involves cutting the pattern, spreading the pieces apart, and forming darts to remove excess fabric where necessary.

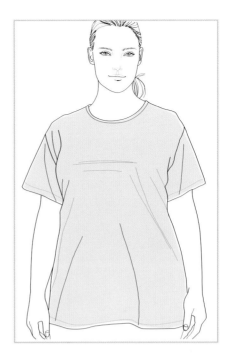

Dartless or seamless top

A top without any shaping will lie awkwardly over the figure and may generally look too large or pull across the bust and show excess fabric under the bust and over the shoulders. Use stretch fabric with darts to create a better fit.

3 Tape paper to the sleeve seam on the front and add the same amount to allow the sleeve to fit the enlarged armhole. It is not ideal to add extra material to the sleeve where it may not be required, but the enlarged side seam makes this necessary.

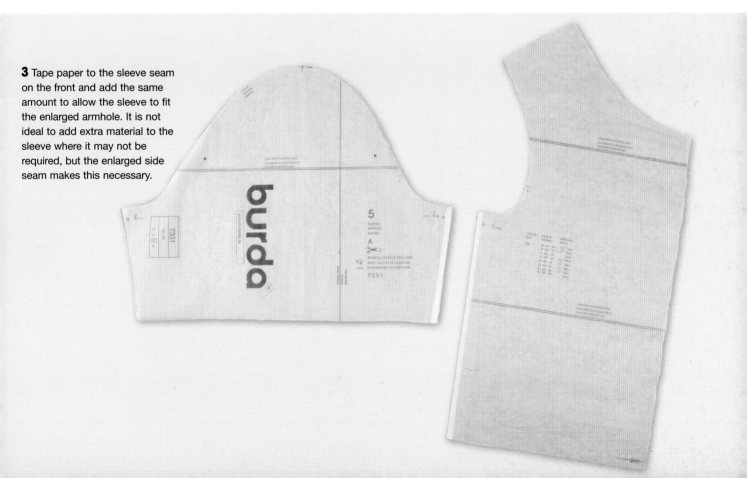

Adding darts to create shape

Adding darts to a shapeless top improves its fit and appearance.

Preparation: Measure across the fullest part of your bust (from side to side), keeping the tape measure level. Divide this figure by two to give the measurement from the center front to the side seam. Cut out the front pattern piece in the appropriate size according to your frame and not your bust measurement.

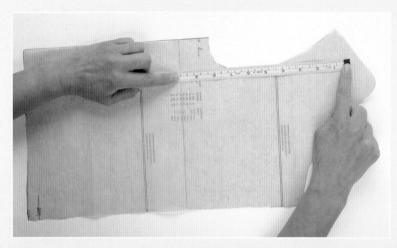

1 Take the measurement from your shoulder to your bust level, and draw a horizontal line on the pattern to represent this.

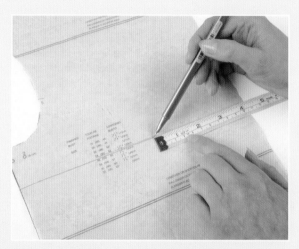

2 Measure from your bust point to the center of your body and mark this point on the pattern.

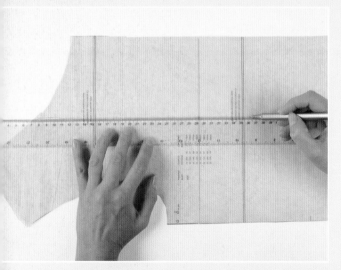

3 Draw a vertical line, parallel to the center front, from the bust point to the hem and also to the middle of the shoulder or neckline (depending on the style of the pattern).

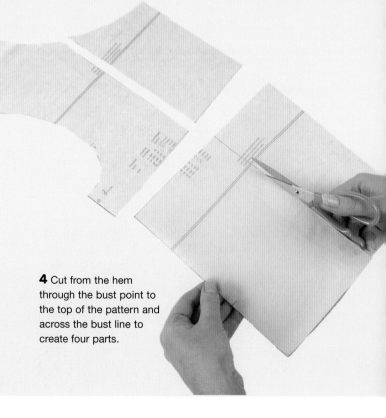

4 Cut from the hem through the bust point to the top of the pattern and across the bust line to create four parts.

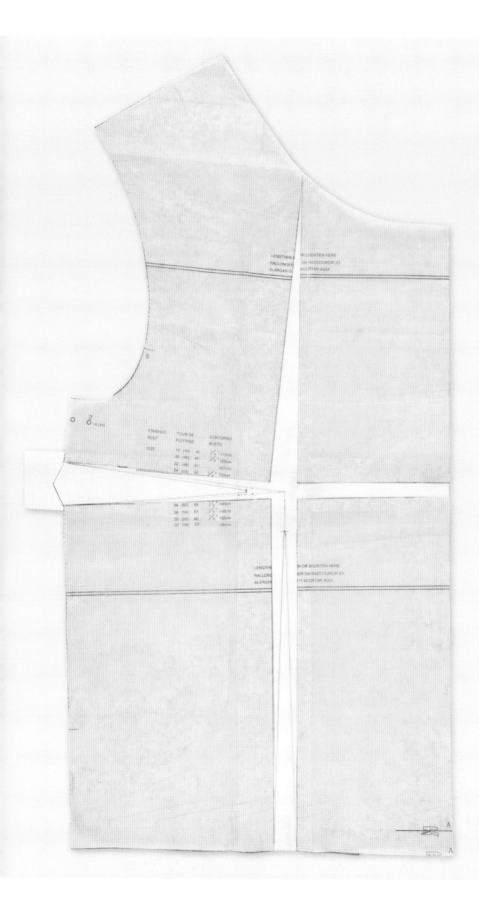

5 Move the two lower pattern pieces down for more horizontal length. Pivot at the top, swinging the armhole out to increase the measurement at bust level to the amount required. Move the lower side piece out and level with the armhole above it. The side will slide out, increasing the width of the pattern at the hem.

6 Place paper below the pattern and tape to hold in place. Draw lines on the separated pattern from the hem to the bust point and from the side seam to the bust point. Mark points 1 in (2.5 cm) short of the bust point and draw in the darts.

Note: Once these darts are created, use the information on pages 74–75 to move them to your preferred position or translate them into a seam if necessary.

Widened back
A good fit across the back of a garment makes it look and feel great.

Back: Broad and narrow back alterations

A good fit across the back of a jacket or dress is essential not only for comfort, but for it to look good too. By simply removing some of the fullness or cutting and sliding the pattern pieces apart, we can improve the fit and make the back panel of a garment look much better. Adapting the pattern before cutting out the fabric is time well spent in achieving a snug fit with sufficient ease and a smooth, wrinkle-free finish.

The first step is to assess the correct measurements to work with. A bust measurement is the circumference of the body at the widest part of the bust. This, however, does not indicate whether the measurement consists of a broad back and small bust, or a narrow back and larger bust. If you are aware that you have a particularly narrow or broad back, get someone to help you to take these measurements and compare them with the

Adapting a pattern for a broad back

If a jacket or dress is too tight across the back, it will be uncomfortable to wear and may give the impression of being too small, even if the garment fits well elsewhere. Extending the pattern in the upper back is the answer to this problem and will not affect the fit at the lower back.

Preparation: You will need the back bodice pattern piece(s) cut out in the most appropriate size. Have your own back measurement handy to compare with the pattern.

1 Measure from the center back to mid-armhole on the pattern, omitting the seam allowances. Compare this with you own measurement. The difference will be the amount you need to add to give a good fit.

2 Draw a line vertically through the shoulder to a point 1 in (2.5 cm) below the armhole. Draw a second line horizontally from here to the side seam.

3 Cut along the lines to separate the armhole from the bodice.

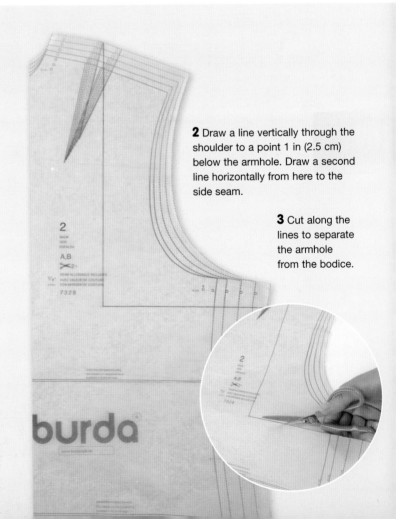

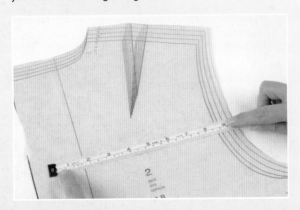

detailed standard measurements on the pattern envelope. This will let you see whether an alteration is likely to be needed at the pattern stage or if a small adjustment will do the trick when the garment is sewn. Small modifications can be made in the center-back seam of a jacket or dress, but for a larger adjustment, the back pattern must be cut and moved to accommodate the change. If the back panel is too small, there is the chance the seams will be under pressure and stitches may break as a result.

To adapt the back panel and add width, cut vertically through the middle of the shoulder and horizontally under the armhole from the side seam, and cut a segment from the back pattern piece. Slide this section out and away from the body of the pattern to increase the back measurement. Once the cutting lines have been smoothed out and any affected darts straightened, the pattern is ready to cut in fabric. The resulting jacket or dress has more fabric to cover the broader back measurement.

Broad back

If there is not enough fabric in the back panel of a jacket or dress, the armhole seams will be under stress and likely to split away from the jacket. On a sleeveless dress the back will pull inward. Both garments will look tight and be uncomfortable to wear.

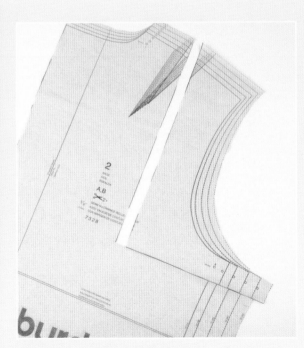

4 Move this piece to the side by the required amount to add room for the broader back. Place paper below it to create the new pattern.

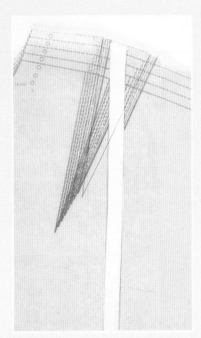

5 Enlarge and reshape the shoulder dart. Find the center of the dart and mark the original length, then draw in the new dart outline. Here we show the original in blue and the new dart in red.

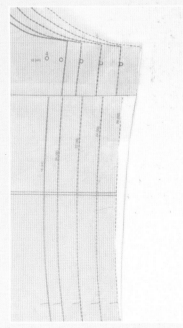

6 Join the line from the underarm to the hem to create a smooth side seam. The pattern is now ready to use.

Adapting a pattern for a narrow back

When there is excess fullness across the back of a garment, it is important to remove it. This will make it easier to wear and improve its appearance. If the style has a center-back seam, or princess seams, the extra fullness can be easily removed. Take the back measurement between the shoulders and compare this to the pattern pieces without the seam allowances, then divide up the excess and take a small amount off each seam. A pattern with shoulder darts can be adapted into a princess-seam style by cutting vertically through the dart to the hem and reshaping where the fabric needs to be removed.

Preparation: You will need the back pattern piece(s) and your own back measurement taken between the shoulder blades. The example pattern has a yoke, but other styles may have a shoulder seam, making them less complicated to deal with.

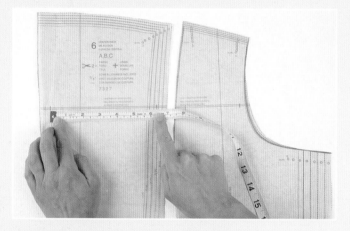

1 Measure across the back from the center back to mid-armhole, omitting the seam allowances.

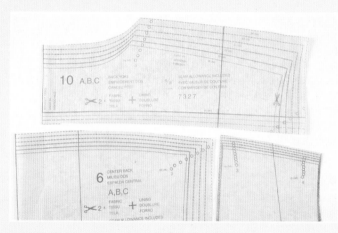

2 Mark the seam position on the yoke and draw a line to the front edge.

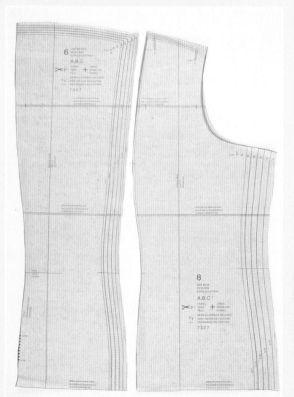

3 Calculate how much fabric must be removed for a comfortable fit, remembering to include some for ease of wear, and divide this amount by the number of seams (in this case, two). Mark this amount at mid-armhole level and smooth a line from waist to shoulder, removing the excess from the back where required. Cut away the excess from the pattern. If your pattern includes seam allowances, the excess cut from the outer cutting line will mean stitching ⅝ in (1.5 cm) inside. This will be the new sewing line.

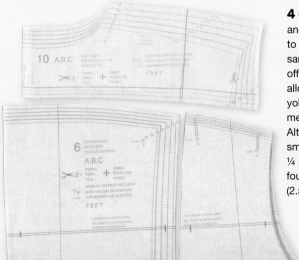

4 Cut into the yoke and pivot the pattern to overlap by the same amount shaved off the back seam allowance so the yoke will fit the newly measured back. Although this is a small amount, ¼ in (6 mm) over four seams is 1 in (2.5 cm) in total.

Sleeve: Adjusting length

One of the areas in which we all differ is the length of our arms, and the wrong sleeve length can be unflattering. A well-fitting jacket, for example, looks completely wrong if the cuff length is too long and hides your fingers, or is too short and exposes too much of your wrist. Getting the sleeve length balanced and in proportion to suit you is easy. By simply cutting and extending the pattern, you add length to the sleeve or you can shorten it by tucking and folding.

This pattern adjustment also applies to three-quarter length and short sleeves, and fine-tuning the length will ensure a perfectly proportioned look. The cuff edge of a traditional Chanel-style jacket, for example, sits just above the wrist in order to show off some beautiful jewelry. On a short-sleeved shirt, if the hem drops below the elbow, this will look unbalanced and make the shirt seem too large.

A small sleeve-length adjustment may be made at the hem. However, to retain the correct proportion, the best way to alter the length is to modify the pattern. This ensures that the cuff circumference is appropriate and does not become too large and that the elbow remains at the right level.

To make an appropriate sleeve length alteration, ask a friend to measure your arm length (see page 19) and compare this with the standard measurement chart of the pattern. Also, check the actual length of the pattern without seam allowances and hems from the top to cuff level. This will indicate how much the sleeve needs to be lifted or lengthened. Tuck away or cut and extend the pattern to the amount required before cutting out your fabric.

Take a little time to make small adjustments in the length to achieve a perfect look.

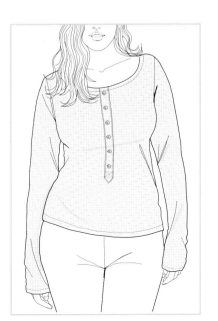

Long sleeves
When the sleeves of a top are too long the general appearance of the outfit is sloppy (left). The hem of the sleeve wrinkles around the wrist and may get in the way. Shorten the pattern before cutting out the fabric rather than taking up the hem of the sleeve at the end to achieve the best finish (above).

Lengthening a sleeve

To lengthen a sleeve and improve the fit of a dress or jacket, look for the double lines marked on the pattern. These indicate where to make the adjustment. If the sleeve has more than one panel, make the same adjustment to all parts.

Preparation: You will need the sleeve pattern piece or pieces and the actual arm length measurement from the outer edge of the shoulder to the length required—use the area between the wrist bone and the top of the hand as a guide.

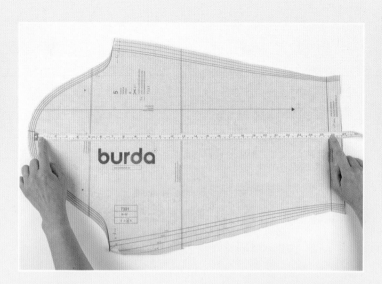

1 Measure from the head of the sleeve to the hem, ignoring the seam allowances. Compare this with your own measurement and make a note of the adjustment required.

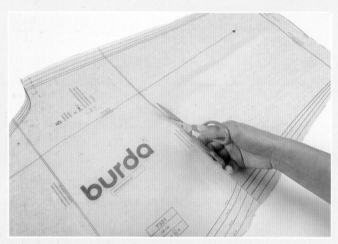

2 Cut through the double lines printed across the sleeve pattern.

3 Slide the pattern pieces apart, keeping them parallel and the outer edges level. Tape the pattern to a piece of paper and tidy up the sleeve seams to make a neat and straight join.

Shortening a sleeve

To shorten the sleeve pattern, reverse the movement of the pattern pieces and make a fold to take up the excess length. Secure with tape or glue and use this modified pattern to cut out your sleeves.

Sleeve: Adjusting the upper arm

While the sleeve may have a generally good fit, sometimes more width is needed in the upper arm for greater comfort. To achieve this extra movement without restyling the sleeve entirely, you need to cut and modify the pattern. It is a fussy task, but well worth the effort for a comfortable finish.

This alteration is not necessary on many sleeve styles, but for a slim-fitting design, extra width can be incorporated if necessary. The pattern is divided up into vertical sections and then cut apart. Move the sections outward, pivoting from the top to retain the size of the sleeve head so it will continue to fit into the armhole. The side seams are redrawn to keep the original circumference at the cuff edge. Because of the reshape, the resulting pattern has a little more ease in the upper arm for a more comfortable fit. If you are using a pattern with more than one piece, pin the parts together before marking the vertical divisions and separate them when the alteration has been made.

Tight upper sleeve
A slim-fitting sleeve is sometimes too tight in the upper arm. This appears as pulling across the top of the arm and makes the shoulder and the head of the sleeve push upward awkwardly. It looks and feels uncomfortable to wear.

Widened upper arm
Alter the sleeve pattern to enlarge the width for an upper arm if required.

Increasing upper arm width in a sleeve

Carry out this alteration to achieve more ease in the upper arm of a tight-fitting sleeve. Be aware that only a small amount of additional ease is created with this method and a different choice of sleeve style may be a better option in some cases.

Preparation: Cut the sleeve pattern from the other pieces and cut it out in the appropriate size. Ask a friend to measure the circumference of your upper arm.

1 Measure the width of the pattern at the underarm point, but do not include the seam allowances. Make a note of the measurement.

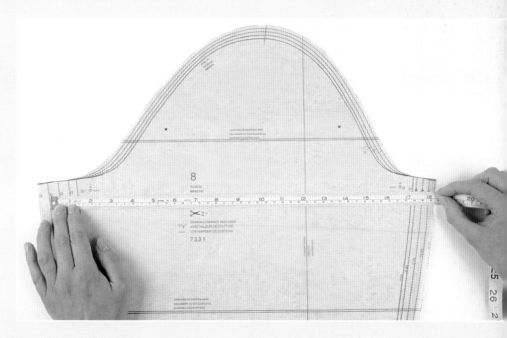

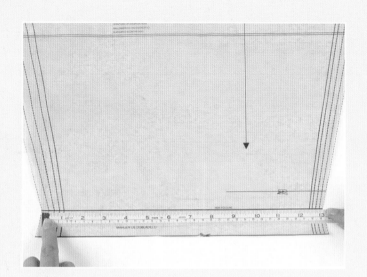

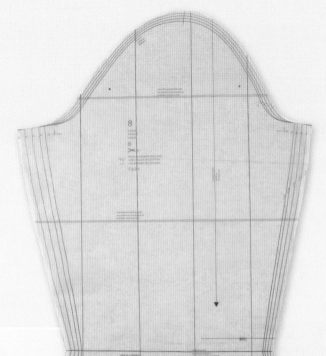

2 Make a note of the measurement of the width at the hem of the sleeve to use later.

3 Divide the sleeve into five equal parts and draw vertical lines through the pattern.

4 Cut through the vertical lines and spread these sections apart, pivoting at the upper edge of the sleeve head. Tape to a piece of paper to hold the newly widened pattern in place. Using the hem measurement taken in step 2, mark this in the center of the hem and redraw the side seams of the sleeve.

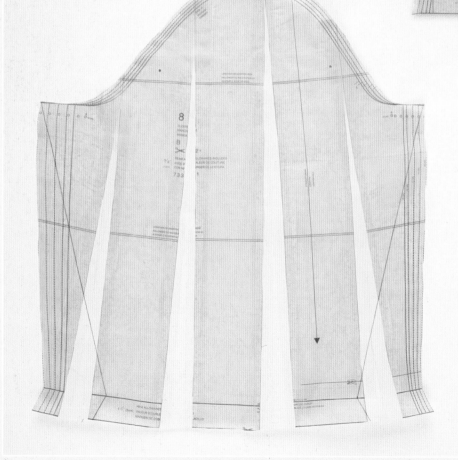

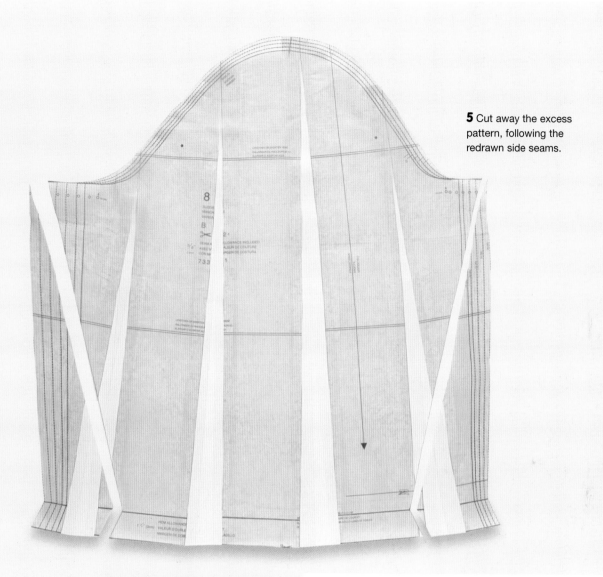

5 Cut away the excess pattern, following the redrawn side seams.

6 Measure the underarm width and check that additional ease has been added to improve the fit of the sleeve.

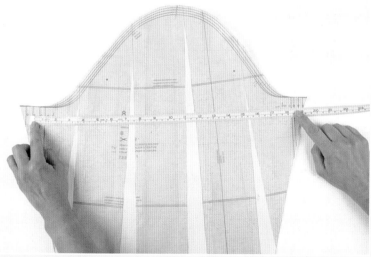

Sleeve: Altering the style

A full range of styles, from slim and fitted to wide and flowing can be created from a basic sleeve pattern. Narrower sleeves involve reducing the width of the pattern, splitting it into a number of panels, and adding an elbow dart. Wider styles are formed by cutting and spreading the pattern pieces. With some design flair, numerous exciting styles can be produced.

Flared sleeve

Adding width to the base of a sleeve rather than the sleeve head produces an elegant draped effect and looks perfect with the right choice of bodice. The fullness is left free to hang at the hem of the sleeve.

Preparation: Trace the sleeve onto pattern paper and cut it to the finished length required. Transfer all the pattern markings.

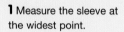

1 Measure the sleeve at the widest point.

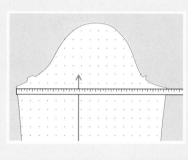

2 Divide the sleeve into six equal sections with vertical lines.

3 Cut along the lines, leaving a tiny hinge at the head of the sleeve. Pivot the sections apart by approximately 2–4 in (5–10 cm) at the hemline, spreading out the sleeve pattern. Tape this to a piece of paper.

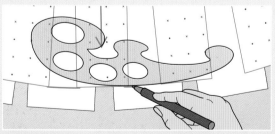

4 Draw in the lower edge of the sleeve (a French curve helps to create a smooth arch) and smooth the sleeve head. Cut away the excess paper.

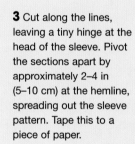

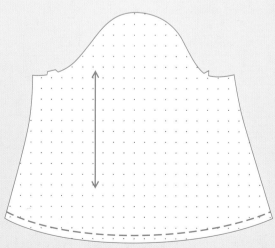

5 Trace the pattern and draw in the grain line parallel to the center of the sleeve. Add a hem allowance to the lower edge.

SEWING

Sew the side seams of the sleeve together and neaten the hem. This is now ready to be inserted into the armhole of the garment.

Closer-fitting sleeve

A closer-fitting sleeve does not, as you might think, make a garment restrictive and less comfortable. In fact, a sleeve cut close to the armhole actually allows more movement. A slimmer-fitting sleeve can be drafted as several parts, but you can adapt a basic one-piece sleeve to improve the shape and fit by dividing it into two panels. Use a basic pattern (without seam allowances), or use a simple fashion sleeve pattern that includes allowances and add seam allowances only to the relevant cut edges at the end.

Two-piece sleeve

Adding a second seam to a basic sleeve creates a narrower silhouette. Cutting higher into the armhole is not described here, but slimming and shaping the sleeve will improve the look.

Preparation: Trace the basic sleeve onto pattern paper and transfer the pattern markings, including the vertical line, through the middle.

1 Mark a point 1¼ in (3 cm) inside the side seam on the hem and reshape the side seams from the underarm.

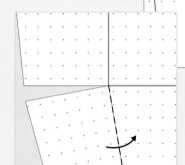

2 At elbow level, cut across to the central vertical line and cut to the center of the hem at the wrist. Pivot this panel, moving it forward 1½ in (4 cm) at the hem opening at the elbow. Secure it to paper with tape or glue.

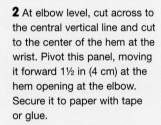

3 Mark a dart at the elbow of half the length less ⅜ in (1 cm).

4 Draw a line from the point of the elbow dart to the hem and to the sleeve head, parallel to the side seam.

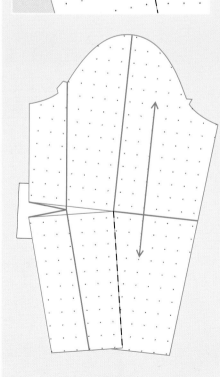

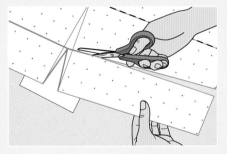

5 Cut along this line and close up the elbow dart. This will help to shape the sleeve when it is sewn.

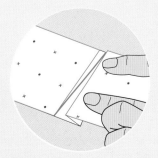

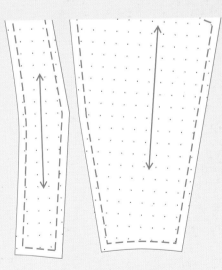

6 Trace the two panels onto pattern paper and add seam allowances to the cut edges. These will become the two panels for the sleeve.

Sleeve: Adding cuffs

If you decide that a plain hem at the end of your sleeve is not how you want to finish your garment, you can easily add a cuff. This has the potential to change the length and silhouette of the sleeve.

Adding a shirt cuff

It is easy to add a cuff, whether deep or narrow, by making a few adjustments. All you need is to choose the depth of cuff you want to complete your sleeve.

Preparation: Trace the sleeve pattern onto pattern paper and transfer the pattern markings. Decide on the depth of the shirt cuff.

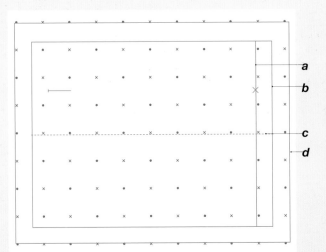

1 To make the cuff pattern:

a Draw a rectangle twice the depth of the finished cuff and the width of the wrist measurement with 2 in (5 cm) added.
b Add a ⅝ in (1.5 cm) extension to one edge for the button and buttonholes.
c Draw the center fold line through the middle and mark the button and buttonhole positions.
d Add a ⅝ in (1.5 cm) seam allowance to all edges.

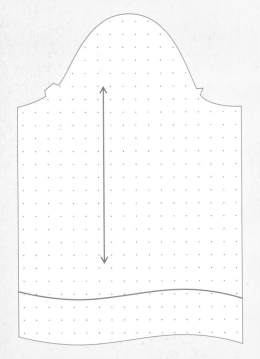

2 Shorten the length of the sleeve by the cuff depth, following the line of the hem.

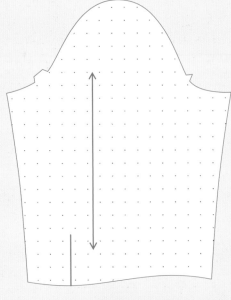

3 Narrow the width of the sleeve at the base by 1½ in (4 cm) and redraw the side seams to the new point on the hem with a slight curve. Mark the placket opening halfway between the center and side seam on the back of the sleeve.

SEWING

Make up the cuffs with suitable interfacing and tuck under the top edges. Create a placket opening and sew the side seams. Make tucks in the lower edge to match the cuff size, then slip the raw edges of the base of the sleeve into the cuff. Topstitch and edge stitch to secure the cuff to the sleeve.

Adding a cuff band

This type of cuff is generally suitable for garments made from stretch fabric. A folded band of plain stretch or ribbed fabric is attached to the lower edge of the sleeve to neaten it and form a border. No fastenings are required as the fabric extends and eases over the hand when being pulled on or taken off. It is a method used in manufacturing yet easily reproduced at home.

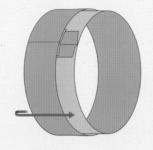  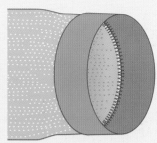

1 Use a matching ribbed fabric or the same stretch material as the garment for the cuff band. Measure the lower circumference of the sleeve and cut your cuff band approximately 1 in (2.5 cm) shorter than this (the band must be shorter than the sleeve to hold it firmly when finished). For a 2 in (5 cm) deep cuff cut it 5 in (12 cm) wide. With right sides together, sew the band into a tube then fold in half, enclosing the raw edges inside.

2 Mark both the cuff and sleeve into quarters and pin these together with right sides facing, then sew on the seam line through all layers; for best results use a serger, but if one is not available set the sewing machine to stretch stitch.

3 Pull the cuff downward and the seam allowance up toward the top of the sleeve to finish.

Alternative cuff choices

You can change the look of a plain sleeve by altering the style of the cuff. This is a chance to be creative.

Double shirt cuff

To make the double-cuff pattern, draw a rectangle four times the depth required and the width of the wrist measurement with 2 in (5 cm) added. Add a further ⅝ in (1.5 cm) to each end for the buttonholes. Draw the fold lines across the cuff and mark the buttonhole positions. Finally, add seam allowances and cut one cuff per sleeve.

Shaped cuff

Draw a rectangle to represent the depth of the cuff by the measurement of the base of the sleeve. Divide the rectangle into six equal parts, then open them up at the upper edge to create a gentle curve. Add seam allowances to all sides then cut two in fabric, as a cuff and a facing, for each sleeve.

Flounced cuff

Draw a rectangle to represent the depth of the flounce by the measurement of the base of the sleeve. Divide the rectangle into eight equal parts and open up to form a circle, with the inner corners touching. Smooth off the edges and add a ¼ in (6 mm) seam allowance to the inner and outer edges.

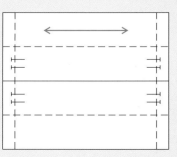

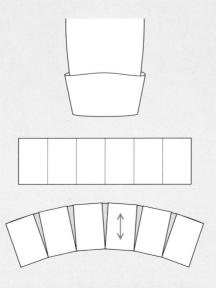

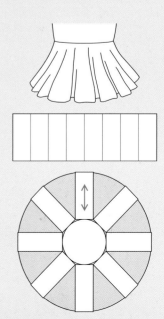

Sleeve: Altering to match the armhole

When making alterations to improve the fit of the armhole, shoulder, and back, you may need to adjust the shape and size of the sleeve head. Without making these changes, the sleeve will not fit neatly into the bodice, leaving untidy gathers in the top of the sleeve if the sleeve head is too big, or unnatural tucks in the shoulder or bodice if it is too small. Make sure the bodice fits well, then make the appropriate changes in the sleeve pattern to match.

Drafting a sleeve pattern

The sleeve pattern is originally drafted by the pattern maker using the size of the armhole of the bodice. This is measured and the sleeve is drafted onto it using the shape and angle of the curves so that the two will fit perfectly when joined. The upper part of the sleeve—the head or cap—is a convex curve on the sleeve, while the under arm area is concave. The points where the curves meet, for the upper- and underarmhole and sleeve, are often marked on the front and back of both the sleeve and bodice patterns, or sometimes just at the front.

When to adapt the sleeve pattern

The sleeve pattern must be adapted if any part of the bodice has been altered. It may be that the underarm has been lowered to make the bodice less restrictive, and in this case the sleeve will require an alteration under the arm for it to continue to fit. If the armhole is taken in to remove gaping at the side of the bust, the sleeve alteration must be made to the lower front sleeve edge. When a shoulder adjustment is made, by either lowering or raising the angle, the head of the sleeve has to be adapted too. Match the position from the bodice and sleeve pattern pieces for an appropriate alteration. If fullness is added or removed in the wrong area, the sleeve fit will not look natural when sewn.

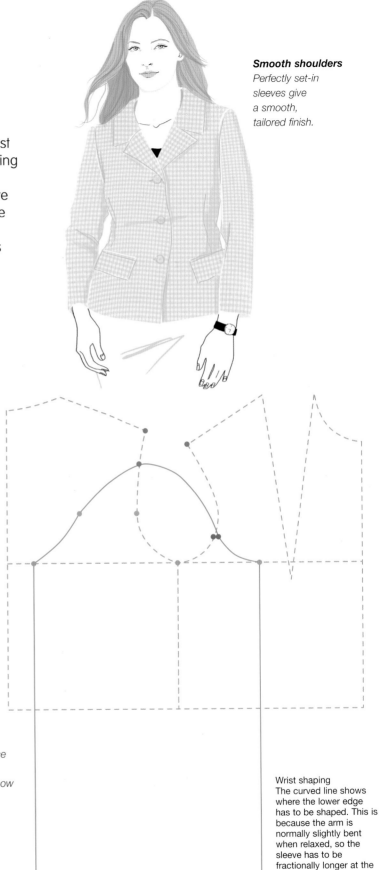

Smooth shoulders
Perfectly set-in sleeves give a smooth, tailored finish.

Sleeve pattern
The sleeve is drafted from the bodice pattern. Balance points on both the bodice and sleeve are marked to show where they are matched when the sleeve is inserted.

- ● Sleeve head
- ● Back armhole balance points
- ● Front armhole balance points
- ● Underarm seam

Wrist shaping
The curved line shows where the lower edge has to be shaped. This is because the arm is normally slightly bent when relaxed, so the sleeve has to be fractionally longer at the back than the front.

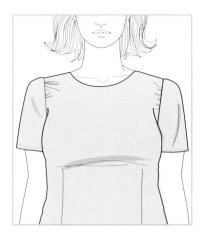

Wrinkled bodice

If the bodice alteration is made without changing the sleeve, the armhole may be larger on the bodice than the sleeve. This would create wrinkles around the side of the bodice where it gathers unnaturally at the armhole. Reshape the underarm of the sleeve to give a smooth seam.

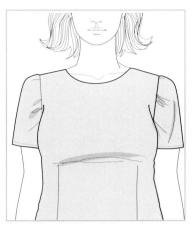

Bulging sleeve

If the bodice alteration is made without changing the sleeve pattern, there may be excess fabric in the sleeve at the front. This has to be eased into the bodice in order to fit and will balloon from the seam. To prevent this, reshape the sleeve before cutting out in fabric.

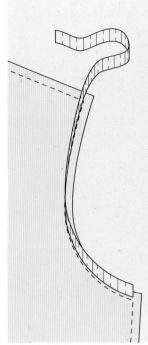

Measuring the seam line

Patterns are drafted without seam allowances; these are added later. When you buy patterns, the seam allowances are generally included. This means that the outer edge of the sleeve will not be the same length as the armhole outline. To check whether the sleeve and armhole are compatible, always measure on the seam line, ⅝ in (1.5 cm) inside the cutting line.

Altering the underarm and sleeve

If the underarm has been lowered or raised to improve the fit of the bodice, the sleeve pattern must be adapted to match. Here, instructions are given for lowering the armhole. If you need to raise the armhole, reverse the directions.

Preparation: Collect the bodice pattern pieces with the amendments marked and cut out the sleeve pattern in the correct size. The amended outside edge is the cutting line and the sewing line is ⅝ in (1.5 cm) inside this.

1 Trace the shape of the amended armhole line on the front and back bodice pieces. Use a French curve to give you a neat line if you like.

2 Place the front sleeve over the front bodice and trace through the line at the altered armhole. Use a French curve to create a neat line.

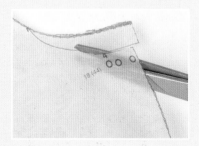

3 Cut along the newly shaped line.

Modifying a sleeve to match an altered bodice

Where the front of the bodice has been adapted because of gaping at the bust, the sleeve pattern must be altered too. Without an alteration, the sleeve would be larger than the armhole and some tucks would be required for the two pieces to fit.

This alteration may have been made on the bodice pattern but, more likely, will have arisen at the toile stage. If this is the case, transfer the required adjustment from the toile back onto the pattern before continuing. The modification is usually transferred to the nearest seam or dart, so this is the focus of the sleeve alteration.

Preparation: Cut out the relevant bodice pattern pieces and the sleeve in the appropriate size.

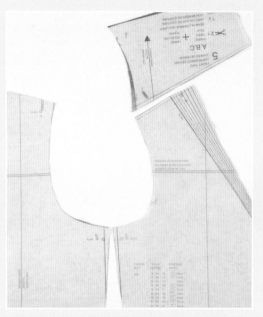

1 Examine the bodice and check where changes have been made. In this example, the side seam has been taken in and the yoke seam reduced.

2 Remove the same amount from the under-sleeve seam to match the bodice alteration.

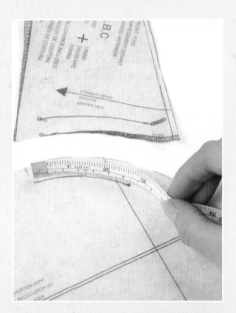

3 Find the point on the sleeve head to match the yoke seam. If there is no pattern marking to show this, measure from the shoulder point with the tape (on its side) on the seam line to find the correct position.

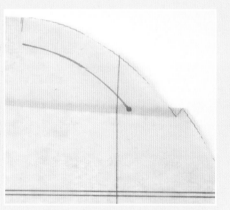

4 Make a tuck to remove the fullness at the front of the sleeve equal to the yoke seam alteration. Leave the back of the sleeve as is.

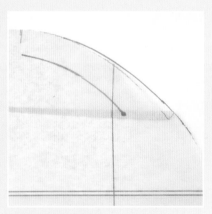

5 Secure the sleeve pattern with tape and reshape the sleeve at the armhole edge if necessary. The pattern is now ready to use.

Waist: Adjusting darts

A well-fitting skirt is a dream to wear. It does not ride up, slip down, dig in, or gape at the back—it just molds comfortably to your body. Achieving a perfectly fitted skirt starts by cutting out the size closest to your own and then fine-tuning by adjusting the darts to fit your body.

What type of dart do you need?

A straight skirt is essentially a cylinder with shaped side seams and darts at the waist to remove excess material. Depending on your figure type, the number, position, shape, and length of these darts will vary. An hourglass figure will require short, deep darts to shape the fabric from the wider hip to the narrower waist. An apple-shaped or rounder figure may need very little definition at the waist with fewer, narrower darts. With this in mind, a number of figure types may choose the same skirt pattern in the same size because their waist and hip measurements are the same, but they will require entirely different kinds of darts.

Pattern markings show darts as a series of dots in a "V"-shape, which are transferred to fabric with chalk, pens, or tailor's tacks. Having taken time to accurately transfer the information from pattern to fabric, it would seem obvious to match these and sew as a straight line through the markings. However, as we are all contoured differently, we should sew the darts according to our body shape for a smooth finish and comfortable fit.

Waist darts
For a good, smooth fit, consider the length and shape of waist darts.

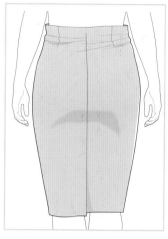

Narrow waist in relation to hip
When the waist is small compared to the hip measurement, as with a pear-shaped figure, there will be extra fabric at the waist. This can result in the skirt twisting out of place or unsightly wrinkles at the waist. Increasing the amount of fabric taken at each dart and seam will improve the fit.

Dart shaping

Choose an appropriate dart shape for your figure type.

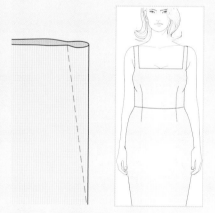

Narrow, straight dart
For straight, column figures with a broad waist in comparison to the hip measurement, a narrow, straight dart is required because there is little fabric to remove at the waist.

Rounded dart
When weight is carried at the upper hip and the waist is small and defined, a short, rounded dart is needed to reduce the fabric fullness at the waist.

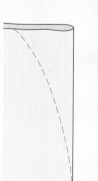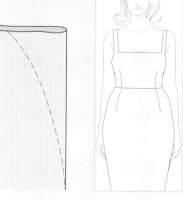

Long and curved dart
Some figure types—pear shapes, for example—have narrow waists and weight carried at the hip bone and bottom, which is some distance below the waist. The dart, therefore, has to be long but also curved to shape a narrower waist.

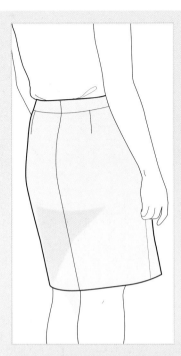

Two-piece waistband

Skirts and pants finished with a two-piece waistband improve the comfort and fit at the back and waist. The angled waistband is tilted inward at the upper edge for a closer fit. This is common in men's pants, but less so for womenswear. Make a seam at the center back of the waistband, and angle the ends of the interfacing band before covering them with fabric. Having a center-back seam in the waistband also makes adjusting at a later stage easier too. This adjustment helps to improve shaping for a narrow waist and also for a hollow back (see page 104).

Shaping for a narrow waist

If you have a relatively slim waist in relation to your hips, you will need to remove more fullness at the waist to achieve a good fit. Without an appropriate pattern alteration, your skirt will be loose at the waist and may even shift out of place.

Preparation: Cut out the front and back pieces of the skirt pattern, using your hip measurement as a size guide. Take your waist measurement.

1 Measure the waist on the sewing line (not the pattern edge) of the pattern pieces, omitting the seam allowances and darts.

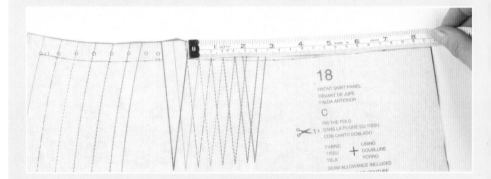

$$\frac{\text{pattern waist measurement} - \text{body waist measurement and ease}}{\text{number of sides of each dart and seam}} = \text{alteration}$$

2 Subtract your own waist measurement and ease from the pattern measurement. This will give the amount you need to increase your darts and side seams by. Divide this measurement by the number of edges of seams and darts. This is the amount that must be added to each side of each dart and seam.

3 Mark the amount at the waist level of each dart and seam and draw in the new waist shape from the hip line and to the point of each dart.

4 To finish, alter the waistband or facing by the same amount.

Adapting for a broad waist

If you have a broad waist in comparison to your hips, a skirt may be tight at the waist without a pattern alteration. In this case, more fabric has to be added at the waist and the darts and seams reshaped accordingly.

Preparation: Select the skirt front and back pattern pieces in a size to suit your hip measurement, but don't cut them out yet. Take your waist measurement.

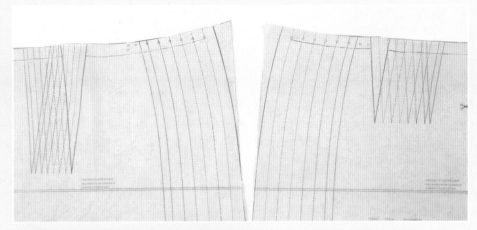

1 Before cutting out the skirt pattern pieces, draw straight, vertical (and parallel) lines from the hip to the waist. This gives extra pattern tissue to make the reshape easier.

2 Measure the actual waist measurement of the skirt, omitting the seam allowances and darts.

3 Subtract the pattern waist measurement from your own to give the amount of extra fabric required at the waist. Divide the measurement calculated by the number of edges of darts and seams. This gives the measurement that must be taken from each seam and dart for a comfortable fit.

$$\frac{\text{body waist measurement and ease} - \text{pattern waist measurement}}{\text{number of sides of each dart and seam}} = \text{alteration}$$

4 Mark the amount inside each dart and outside the side seam, and reshape the darts and seams to give a natural smooth line from hip to waist.

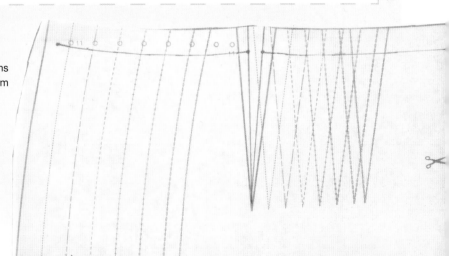

Waist: Hollow back

A hollow back is a common feature of the female figure. As a result the fabric sags and wrinkles below the waist at the small of the back. Excess fabric sits at the lower back, between waist and hip, and must be removed for a smooth finish. This is done by cutting through the pattern at the upper back of the skirt, then reducing the back length. This gives a shorter back length in the skirt to suit the curve of the lower back, but retains the length of the side seam where it is needed.

Don't cut corners

At first sight, it may seem that the easiest way to approach the problem of a hollow back is to cut the excess length from the top of the waist of the back skirt. This shortens the back length and the darts, but the darts are now too narrow and will not remove sufficient fullness from the waist. Taking more time and cutting through and moving the pattern, then smoothing the line of the darts and center-back seam, gives a much better fit.

To assess the amount of fabric to be removed for a hollow back, the most accurate method is to sew a toile and pin out the excess (see page 139). This measurement is then used for the pattern alteration.

Well-fitting skirt back
Adjust the pattern back for a smooth and comfortable fit.

Adapting a pattern for a hollow back

If your skirts and pants fit well at the front but sit awkwardly at your lower back between waist and hip (with extra folds and wrinkles of fabric), it is likely that you have a hollow back. Adapt your pattern before cutting out the fabric to achieve a skirt with a smooth and comfortable fit.

Preparation: Make a toile (see page 136) and calculate the amount of fabric to remove at the skirt back. Cut out the back skirt pattern piece in the appropriate size for your waist and hip.

1 Draw a diagonal line from the waist at the side seam to a point approximately 3 in (7.5 cm) below the waist at the center-back seam and cut along it. Do not cut right through the side seam.

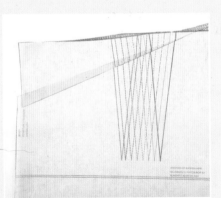

2 Drop the waist at the center back to the amount required and pivot from the side seam. Tape or glue the pattern alteration in its new position.

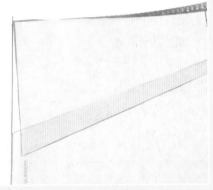

3 Reshape the center-back seam.

4 Redraw the darts in their new length, but original width, so that the skirt will fit at the waist.

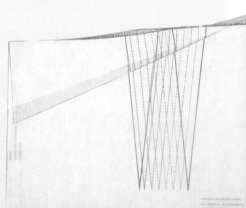

Uneven hips

When one hip is higher or larger than the other, the skirt pulls up at the side seam on both the front and back, with wrinkles pointing toward the larger hip. This also causes the hem to be uneven.

Hips: Uneven hips

Although the human figure appears to be symmetrical, when you look more closely this may not be so. This is sometimes the case for the hips—one hip may be larger, smaller, higher, or lower than the other. The effect of having unbalanced hips is that creases are apparent at hip level on one side of the skirt and the hem is uneven, lifting at one side.

Pattern alteration methods

Rather than straightening the hem of the finished skirt or dress, a much better result can be achieved by altering it at the waist, hip, and side seam. Leveling the hem does not improve the way the skirt hangs at the hem, since the grain will not be straight all around its circumference. Making an adjustment at the waist to extend the side seam and increase the length of fabric sitting around and over a larger hip allows the hem to hang level all the way around.

To carry out an appropriate alteration for one high or large hip, judge how much additional length is required and extend the relevant side seam. Cut horizontally through the high hip level of the skirt from the side seam to the center front and raise this on the side seam, pivoting from the center front. This gives more fabric that will run over the larger hip and down the side seam to the hem, keeping it level with the opposite side seam.

Smooth hip outline

A simple alteration creates a perfect finish over the hip.

Tip

To assess the extra length to add to the larger hip, either measure it directly on the body or make a toile to determine how much more fabric is needed (see page 136). To take the body measurement, tie one length of soft elastic around the waist and a second around the hip at the widest part, making sure it is parallel to the floor. Stand in front of a mirror, and with the help of a friend, measure each side from waist to hip. The difference between the measurements indicates the amount required to add to the side with the larger hip.

Adapting for one high hip

To alter a skirt pattern to make provision for one hip being higher than the other, you must adjust the hip and waist of the pattern on one side only. Since the body is not symmetrical with a higher hip, the skirt pattern pieces cannot be dealt with as one half, so a whole skirt pattern must be created. Use the original standard pattern pieces and add pattern paper to produce a second half.

Preparation: Cut out the front and back skirt pattern pieces in the required size and have pattern paper at hand. Calculate the extra length required to raise the pattern for the higher hip.

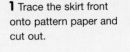

1 Trace the skirt front onto pattern paper and cut out.

2 Find the high hip level on the pattern and draw a line horizontally through the pattern at this point to the center front. Cut through the pattern on this line.

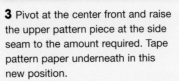

3 Pivot at the center front and raise the upper pattern piece at the side seam to the amount required. Tape pattern paper underneath in this new position.

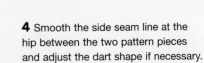

4 Smooth the side seam line at the hip between the two pattern pieces and adjust the dart shape if necessary.

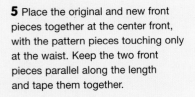

5 Place the original and new front pieces together at the center front, with the pattern pieces touching only at the waist. Keep the two front pieces parallel along the length and tape them together.

6 Cut out a new back in pattern paper and make the same adjustment as you did to the front, extending and reshaping the hip, adjusting the dart(s), and altering the center-back seam.

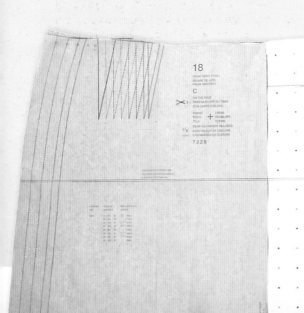

18

FRONT SKIRT PANEL
DEVANT DE JUPE
FALDA ANTERIOR

C

ON THE FOLD
BANDEAU PLIÉE DU TISSU
CON CANTO DE PLIEGO

FABRIC   LINING
TISSU   +   DOUBLURE
TELA   FORRO

SEAM ALLOWANCE INCLUDED
AVEC VALEUR DE COUTURE
CON MARGEN DE COSTURA

7328

Hips: Large thighs

The hip is defined as the widest part around the hip and bottom, and on a standard pattern this is judged to be approximately 7–9 in (17.5–23 cm) below the waist. However, sometimes the thighs, below the hip, protrude more and must be accommodated for a skirt or pants to fit comfortably. If an alteration is not carried out to make room for broad thighs, the fabric will pull and will crease across the front and back of the skirt. It may even ride up and gather around the waist.

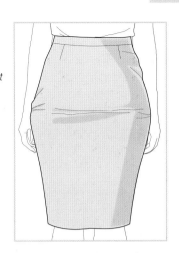

Protruding thighs
A woman with prominent thighs will show fabric pulling across the front and back of a straight skirt, with extra fabric wrinkling above and below the thighs. The skirt is likely to ride up and be tight and uncomfortable to wear.

Adding additional width for large thighs

To alter a pattern to make room for large thighs, additional width has to be introduced at the right level. This is achieved by cutting into the front and back pattern pieces and moving the sections outward to increase the width of the skirt. Finally, reshaping the hip and side seam to create a natural smooth line (see right) completes the modification.

Having added the necessary fabric to the width of the skirt at the thigh level, it is possible that the side seam of the skirt may not perfectly match the outline of the hip and leg. If this is the case, fine-tune the side seam following the instructions for hip reshaping on pages 105–106.

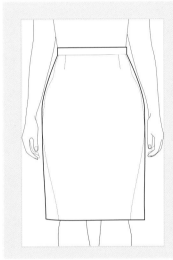

Getting a smooth finish

Do not follow the contour of the hip and thigh faithfully, since the resultant lumpy side seam shows off the thigh bulge rather than concealing it. Instead, draw a natural line that skims the hip and thigh, giving a smooth side seam.

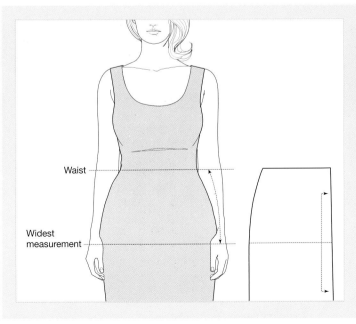

Waist

Widest measurement

Adding additional width for wide hips

The same pattern adjustment is also appropriate for wide hips in cases where it is better to enlarge the hip than reduce the waist measurement. To calculate the amount of extra width needed, whether at the hip or thigh, measure from the waist to the widest part of the hip, and also the circumference at the widest part. This will give you the level at which to expand the pattern and you will be able to determine how much to add to the side seams. Measure the pattern at the level required (omitting the seam allowances) and subtract from your own measurement. Divide the answer by four, for the seams affected, and round this up to the nearest full number to add wearing ease to the skirt or dress. If it remains too tight at thigh level, creases and wrinkles will still appear.

Adapting a pattern for protruding hips or thighs

When wearing a slim-fitting skirt, if the upper thigh is large, it may cause the side seams to bulge outward just below the hip. An alteration to accommodate wider thighs at the pattern stage can correct this fit issue.

Preparation: Cut out the front and back skirt pattern pieces in a size that best suits your hip and waist measurement. Measure your circumference at the widest part of the thigh and measure how far below the waist this is. You will need to know the level at which to expand the pattern and by how much.

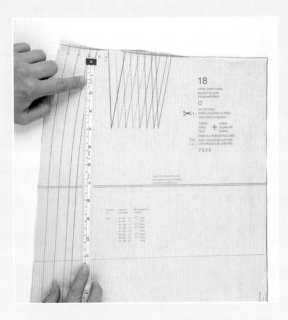

1 On the front pattern piece, measure from the waist to the widest part of the hip/thigh and mark this level.

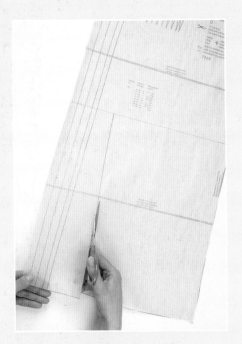

2 Draw a vertical line approximately 3 in (7.5 cm) from the side seam to the hem to the level marked on the pattern. Cut up this line and across to the side seam.

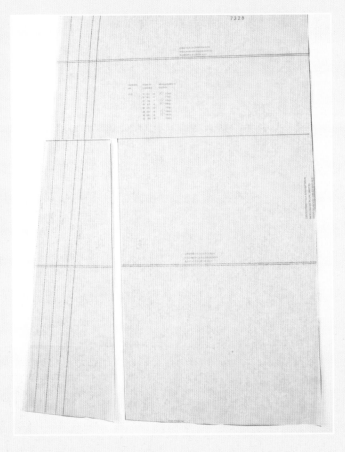

3 Move the section of pattern outward to reach the required width, keeping it parallel to the body of the pattern.

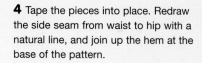

4 Tape the pieces into place. Redraw the side seam from waist to hip with a natural line, and join up the hem at the base of the pattern.

5 Repeat the same process with the back pattern piece and smooth the side seam as you did the front. Finish by fine-tuning the side seam to achieve perfect hip shaping (see page 106).

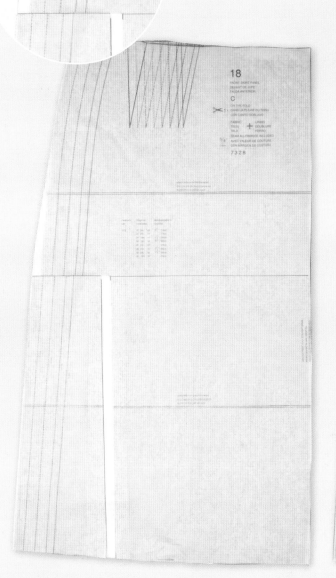

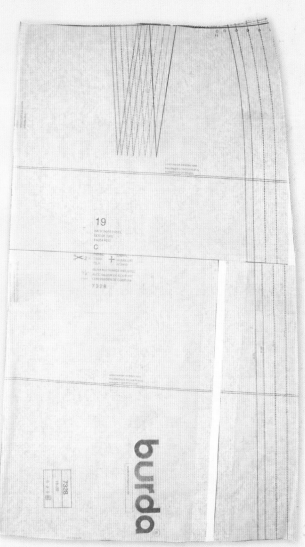

Hips: Large stomach

If you have a large stomach, a skirt or dress will be tight over the front with visible creases drawing attention to the area. The hem will also rise at the front, since the material has farther to travel over the fullness of the front of the body. The poor fit of the skirt or dress will be obvious and it will be uncomfortable to wear because of the tightness around the middle.

The power of pattern adaptations

While Spandex/Lycra-controlled underwear does wonders for the figure, it is not always comfortable to wear. By making clothes to suit your individual shape, you can conceal some bumps and lumps by accommodating them wisely with pattern adaptations.

Incorporate more fabric

Leveling the hem by dropping the front or raising the back will not improve the look of the garment. It is better to incorporate more fabric in the stomach area with a pattern modification. Shortening the darts may help with a small stomach bulge, but it will not be enough to help where it is larger and protrudes, so more fabric must be added to the front skirt panel.

Increasing the size of the front of the skirt is achieved by cutting horizontally across the front of the pattern at mid-stomach level and cutting vertically from the hem to the waist, dissecting the dart. The pattern sections are moved upward and outward to create extra length to cover the protruding stomach, and the dart automatically opens to take up the change in contour of the front of the body. In this pattern alteration, the side seam will be reshaped but the length will remain the same, so no alterations to the back panels are required. The adapted front pattern allows additional fabric to be included to cover the stomach both sideways and vertically over the front, and will continue to fit the rest of the body well.

Adapting a pattern for a protruding stomach

Your waist and stomach tend to broaden with age, unless you spend many hours in the gym keeping them in control. When the stomach becomes large enough to distort the shape of your skirts by pulling across the front and disturbing the hem level, a simple alteration will solve the matter.

Preparation: Cut out the skirt front pattern piece in an appropriate size for your waist and hip measurements. Have some pattern paper handy for your alteration.

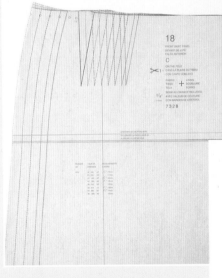

1 Draw two lines through the skirt front; horizontally across the front through the area of concern, and vertically from waist to hem through the dart. Cut along these lines.

2 Move the side panels outward, keeping them parallel, to add space for the vertical enlargement. A protruding stomach requires the front of the skirt to be both longer and wider.

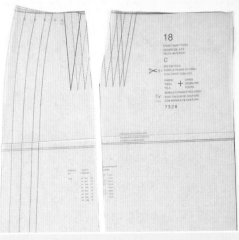

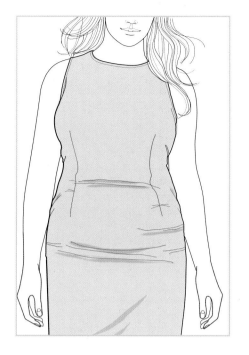

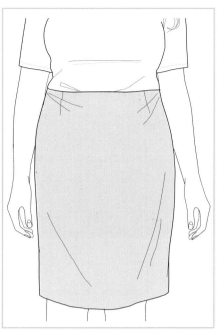

Large stomach

Where the stomach is large, the skirt is tight across the front with horizontal creases over, below, and to the sides of it (far left). The hem level becomes distorted, causing it to rise at the front, since the material has farther to travel up and over the skirt front.

A dropping front hem

If the hem level dips at the front of your skirt, (left) it is possible that the stomach and waist measurements are the same so the front skirt panel has nothing to support it. In this case, cut across the front pattern in the same way as for the large stomach alteration, but reverse the movement of the pieces. Although this is basically the modification for a flat stomach, if you have a larger frame, a broad waist creates the effect of a flat stomach.

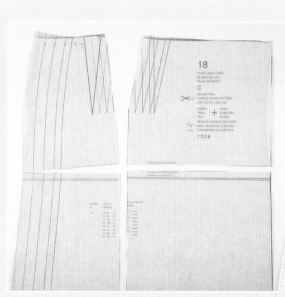

3 Move the center front upward, to accommodate the size of the stomach, keeping the center-front line straight, and tilt the side front upward to meet it, pivoting at the side seam. This ensures that the side seam remains the same length and that the extra fabric is only added where it is needed.

4 Tape or glue the newly positioned pattern pieces to paper to hold them in place. The side seam now has a slight dimple, so reshape it to form a smooth line. Draw the amended dart from center point at the original length to the waist line.

Flattering curves
Make the most of your figure by altering the pattern to work with your body.

Hips: Protruding bottom

Bottoms come in all shapes and sizes, irrespective of your figure type and build. Yours may be small, large, round, flat, or protruding, and you may wish to show it off or conceal it under your clothing. If it protrudes, you will need to carry out a pattern adaptation to increase the amount of fabric in this area of the garment.

Adding additional fabric

The additional fabric is needed to cover the larger seat in all directions; increasing either the length or width on their own is not sufficient. Without a modification, the skirt will be tight over the seat and the side seams may even be strained, stretching the threads in the weave and pulling the stitching. The hem will also rise and hang limply at the back where the fabric is too short to cover the full length from the waist. Additional fabric incorporated into the area of the skirt back will address this problem and a level hem will be achieved.

Adapting a pattern for a large bottom

A larger bottom requires more fabric in the skirt back to fully encompass the body shape. Adapt the back pattern piece before cutting out the fabric and constructing the skirt to avoid disappointment and a need for a more difficult modification when sewn.

Preparation: You will need the back skirt piece cut out in the appropriate size and some pattern paper to hold the adjustment in place.

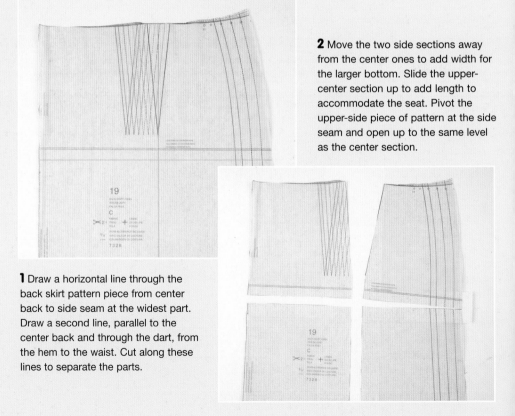

1 Draw a horizontal line through the back skirt pattern piece from center back to side seam at the widest part. Draw a second line, parallel to the center back and through the dart, from the hem to the waist. Cut along these lines to separate the parts.

2 Move the two side sections away from the center ones to add width for the larger bottom. Slide the upper-center section up to add length to accommodate the seat. Pivot the upper-side piece of pattern at the side seam and open up to the same level as the center section.

The alteration required to fix a skirt pattern to suit a large bottom is similar to that of a protruding stomach (see page 110) but the modification is made to the back pattern rather than the front. The pattern is cut both horizontally and vertically and moved out to introduce more space in the pattern to accommodate the large seat without interfering with the waist measurement. The additional fabric covers the body and allows the hem to hang level, doing away with the tightness of the fabric over the seat and giving a straight hem.

The amount of modification a pattern needs to accommodate a large seat is difficult to determine and often comes down to your own judgment. Look at yourself in a full-length mirror and measure from side seam to side seam across the bottom at the widest point and compare this with the back pattern pieces. Spread the pattern pieces to an appropriate distance apart. Modify the pattern as described here and, if necessary, fine-tune the fit at the toile stage to create a perfectly shaped side seam, which follows the contours of the hip (see page 139).

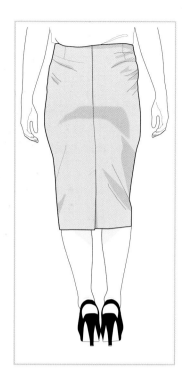

Large bottom

Where the seat is too large for the skirt, creases appear at the sides as well as over and under the bottom. Strain is put on the side seams, causing the weave to be pulled out of shape and the stitching to be under stress. In addition, the back of the skirt may stick out, and the hem will be shorter at the back and will drop lower at the front.

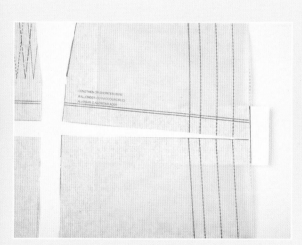

3 Tape the newly positioned pattern pieces to paper to secure the alteration, and reshape the side seam to give a smooth line. Without this, an unsightly indentation would occur in the side seam when the skirt is sewn.

4 Draw in the dart from the new point in the center of the pattern pieces to the original positions at waist level. The dart will be the same length as before, but wider.

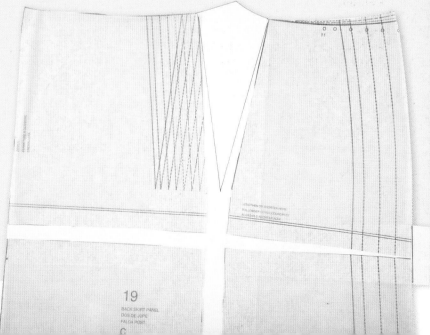

Hips: Flat bottom

The female body comes in every shape and size imaginable, and this is never truer than when referring to the behind. A large, round, and protruding seat requires additional fabric to cover the contours, but some women have a straighter silhouette with no rear at all. The flat seat may coincide with a broad waist and straight hips, but may also be combined with curvy hips, with the weight distributed at the sides rather than the back. The combinations are unlimited, but it is quite possible to adapt a pattern to suit any flat bottom by simple pattern manipulation.

Removing excess fabric from the pattern

A flat bottom poses a problem when fitting, since there is nothing to fill the area and loose fabric lies limply across the back of the skirt. The hem of the skirt will also dip lower at the back than the front, since there is nothing to support the shape. For a figure with a flat seat, the excess fabric at the back of a skirt must be removed for it to hang well on the body. The excess material cannot just be taken into the side seam to remedy this, and leveling the hem from the base is not acceptable either. Modify the basic pattern by cutting it up and sliding the pattern pieces over themselves to reduce the fabric volume in the seat.

Once the modification has been made to the back skirt pattern, the fabric can be cut and the skirt constructed as normal, giving a good fit with a smooth, wrinkle-free finish and a level hem.

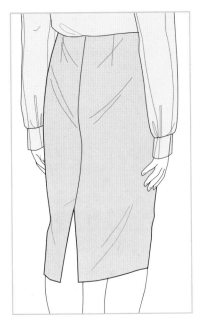

Flat bottom
A flat behind does not fill the back of the skirt and it leaves the fabric loose and saggy in this area. The behind normally fills out the skirt at the back, keeping the hem circumference round and level, but without fullness in the rear, the hem droops limply at the back.

Adapting a pattern for a flat behind

A flat behind leaves skirts baggy and loose in the seat because there is no body fullness to fill the area. Get rid of this surplus material by adapting the pattern and reduce the size of the skirt back pattern before cutting out your fabric. To accurately determine how much fabric you must remove from the rear, make a toile and pin out the excess before transposing these measurements to the pattern (see pages 140–153).

Preparation: You will need the back skirt pattern piece. Cut it out in an appropriate size to fit your waist and hip measurements. There is no need to adapt the front pieces as the side seams of the back, where it meets the front, will remain the same.

1 Draw a horizontal line at the hip level through the back skirt pattern piece from center back to side seam.

2 Draw a second line, parallel to the center back, and through the dart from the hem to the waist. Cut along these lines to separate the parts of the skirt.

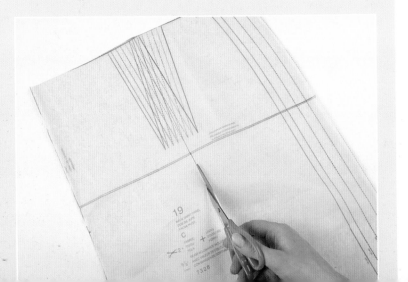

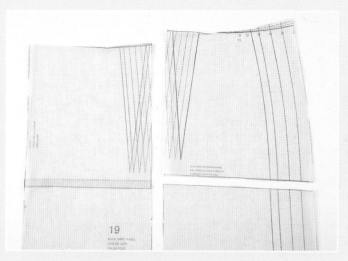

3 Move the upper panel at the center back directly down over the lower section by the amount required to remove the surplus fabric.

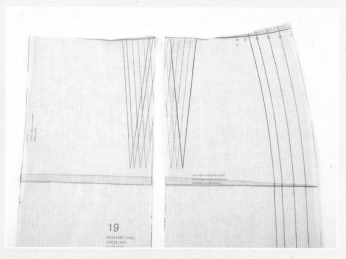

4 Pivot the side section at the hip and slide it down over the lower pattern pieces. The side seam will remain the same length.

5 Overlap the center pieces vertically and tape the pattern pieces in their new configuration. Smooth the outer edge to give a natural seam outline.

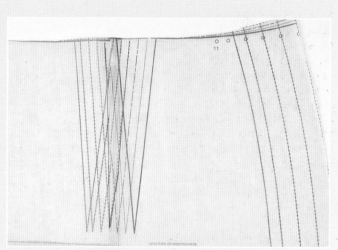

6 Redraw the dart, keeping its original length but making it thinner. This makes sense when you consider that there is less shape to contour because the body has fewer curves; a shallower dart matches the flatter outline required.

Well-fitting pants
*Having a good fit
at the waist of your
pants is essential for
comfort and style.*

Pants: Waist position

We all know the position of our own waist, but this is not always obvious to anyone else. When asked to put your hands on your waist, you will automatically find its natural level, whether you have an hourglass figure with a narrow waist, or a straighter silhouette with fewer curves and a broader middle.

Fashion and waistlines

Although we know where our waistline is, fashion plays its part by raising or lowering it season by season. This is particularly apparent in the design of skirts and pants, sitting high on the waist one season and lower, on the hip bone, another. This does not create a problem for general clothes making, since garments are sized from standard measurements, but it can become an issue when adapting patterns to improve the fit because you need to know what and where to measure. For example, your waist and the top "waist" edge on a pants pattern may not be the same thing. In these cases, you need to find an alternative base line to measure from, and this is usually the hip.

Adapting the waist on low-rise pants

When fitting pants with a low waist level, you cannot compare your waist measurement with the upper edge of the pants pattern because they are different things. You would find that low-rise pants altered to fit your waist measurement would be tight and the hip shape would not be matched to your own. To carry out an accurate alteration, you must determine the level that the pants sit on you and measure your body at this point before starting the adjustment. On the paper pattern, work from the hip and measure the distance above it to the top edge of the pants, then take your own body measurement the same distance above your hip. These are the two measurements you will need to compare to make an accurate alteration. The difference between the two measurements is distributed between the side seams to reshape the waist for a better and more comfortable fit.

Preparation: Take your horizontal body measurement at a level comparable with the pants pattern. Cut out the front and back pants pattern pieces in a size appropriate for your hip and waist measurement.

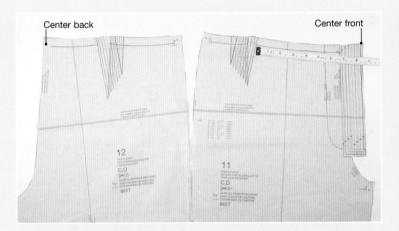

Center back   Center front

1 Place the front and back pattern pieces together on a flat surface and measure the top "waist" edge. Measure on the sewing line ⅝ in (1.5 cm) below the cutting line and omit all seam allowances and darts. Multiply the measurement by two for the full waist measurement.

2 Compare your own measurement with that on the pattern and calculate the difference you will need to add or subtract from the pattern. Divide this figure by four because this is the number of seam edges where the adjustment will be made.

$$\frac{\text{pattern measurement} - \text{body measurement}}{\text{number of seam edges}} = \text{alteration}$$

Finding your waist

You can find your waist by loosely tying a length of elastic around your middle—it will naturally rest at your waist. This is useful when you have a friend helping you take your measurements. It shows them where your waist is and gives a base line from which to take other measurements (see page 19).

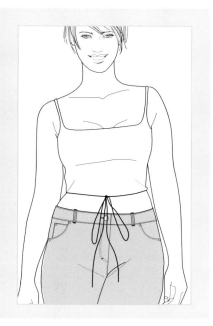

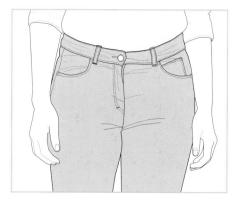

Tight at the waist

Where a model has a broader waist than the pattern, the upper edge is tight and uncomfortable around the torso. The button and buttonhole will be under stress and the top of the zipper placket may gape, revealing the zipper teeth.

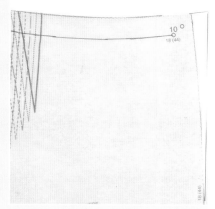

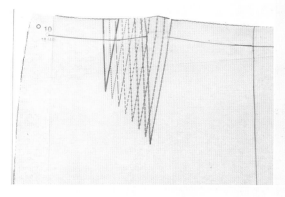

4 Adjust the waistband by the same amount to match the new waist measurement. Cut the waistband pattern and add extra paper to lengthen or make a fold to reduce the length.

3 Enlarge (or reduce) the side seam by the amount calculated in step 2 on the seam line. Add paper to the side seam if enlarging the waist or mark the new position on the existing pattern if reducing it. Draw in the new seam shape. Leave the center-front and center-back seams untouched and ignore the darts.

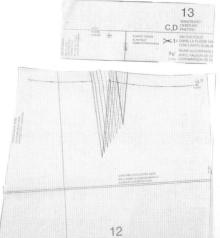

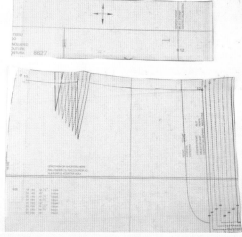

Pants: Broad hips and thighs

Pants are a practical choice for everyday wear, but depending on our figure types, we may not feel comfortable in them if they don't fit well. Finding the right style to suit your frame will make pants appear more chic, and adapting the fit just for you will make them comfortable to wear and look better, too.

Finding the right pants pattern

Finding a well-fitting pair of pants is more difficult than a skirt because it is a more complex pattern shape—having to fit our stomach, seat, and legs all at once. The shape and depth of the crotch is crucial to a comfortable and attractive fit, since it must be deep enough for the body to sit in, but not so large as to look like a sack, and it must fit closely to the body without being too tight. Start with a standard pattern in a size to suit your hips and waist and, if necessary, alter the shape to improve the fit.

Adapting the pants pattern

The initial step to achieving pants that look good and fit well is in the measuring. As well as knowing the waist and hip measurement, the crotch depth is important too (see page 120). Armed with all your measurements, you will be much more likely to achieve a perfect fit. Using the same basic rules as for skirts, cut through the pattern where the fullness is required and spread the pattern sections apart to add the necessary volume, while retaining the length and shape of the outer edges and seams.

Broad hips and thighs

The fabric at the widest part of the hip or thigh is pulled tight, causing creasing from the side seam above and below the bulge. This may, in turn, pull the center-back seam, causing discomfort as the crotch rides up.

Broad hips and thighs

To make provision for larger hips and thighs in pants, enlarge the pattern in the upper leg on the side seam. By adjusting both the front and back pattern pieces, the side seam retains its position. If the back piece alone is enlarged, the side seam shifts forward. If the alteration is to accommodate a large bottom rather than broad hips, increasing the size of the back alone is more appropriate.

Preparation: Establish the broadest level of the hip or thigh and where this sits in relation to the hip level of the pattern. Cut out the front and back pattern pieces in the standard size to best fit your waist and hip.

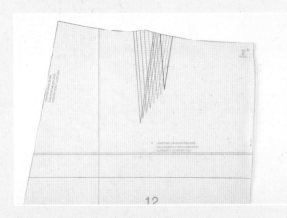

1 Draw a line through the widest part of the hip/thigh from the center-back seam to the side seam.

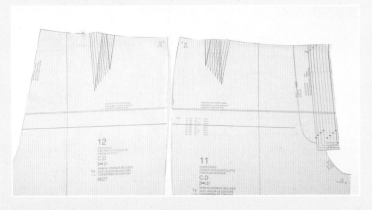

2 Mark the same level on the pattern front and continue this line to the center-front seam.

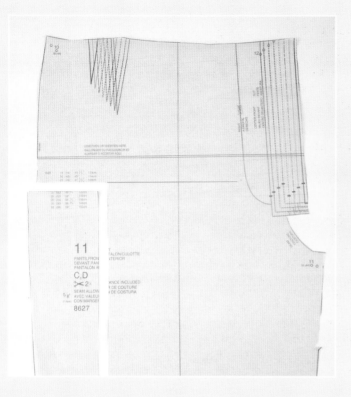

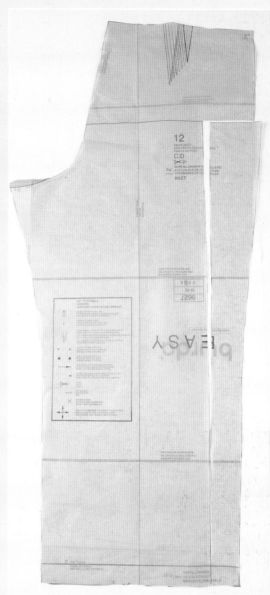

3 Mark a point approximately 3 in (7.5 cm) from the side seam on the horizontal line on both the front and back pattern pieces. Draw lines from here to the hem and cut away this section on both pieces.

4 On both the front and back, pivot the cut section outward from the hem so that the pattern opens at the hip to the required amount and tape in place to paper below. Straighten the hem on the front and back pattern pieces where the cut section was adjusted.

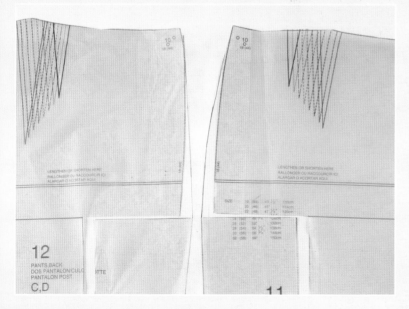

5 Shape the side seam from the top corner of the lower section that has been moved outward, bringing it smoothly into the waist in a natural hip-shaped curve. This new side seam will accommodate the larger hip or thigh but maintain the original waist measurement.

Pants: Crotch

The crotch measurement is probably the most important measurement when fitting pants. If this measurement is wrong, then it may not even be possible to put the pants on to establish if they fit anywhere else. Once you have the pants on, you can at least make a judgment about the fit and alter the seams and waist as necessary.

Measuring the crotch depth

The crotch depth is measured when sitting down—check the distance between the waist and the seat of the chair. This body measurement varies widely in women and matching it can make a huge difference to the fit and comfort of a pair of pants. A more accurate way to measure the crotch is from the waist at the center front to the waist at the center back. So, you are, in fact, measuring the actual distance the crotch seam has to travel in the pants.

However, getting the correct measurement is only part of the solution, since body shape is important, too. You may have a flat rear with a larger stomach so the crotch-seam measurement may need more length at the front rather than the back. Equally, this means that if you have a larger bottom and a flat stomach, the crotch seam must provide more room in the seat and less at the front. For an accurate measurement, take a length of string or ribbon (it must not be stretchy) and tie a knot in the middle. Place the knot between your legs (at the inside seam position) and bring the ends up to meet the front and back waist. Do not pull tight and let the tape sit comfortably as you would want your pants to fit. Mark the back and front waist on the tape with a marker or a pin and use a measuring tape to discover the length. You now have a front and back crotch measurement to compare with the paper pattern so you can make an appropriate alteration.

Crotch too short
The pants show creasing at the top of the legs and at the front and seat where they are tight on the model. They are uncomfortable to wear and must be altered for them to look and feel good.

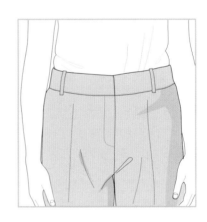

Crotch too long
Excess fabric hangs at the front and back of the pants making them loose, droopy, and unflattering.

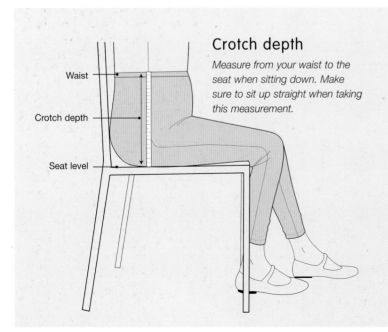

Crotch depth

Measure from your waist to the seat when sitting down. Make sure to sit up straight when taking this measurement.

Waist

Crotch depth

Seat level

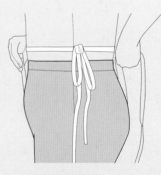

Crotch length

Using a length of ribbon, tie a knot in the middle and place the knot between your legs (at the inside seam position). Pull the ends up to meet the front and back waist, but do not pull tight and let the ribbon sit comfortably as you would want your pants to fit. Once you have marked the back and front waist position on the ribbon, lay it flat and measure it.

Increasing the crotch seam

If pants are tight in the crotch, the seam can be lengthened to give more space to accommodate the body comfortably. This will get rid of any creases or wrinkles around the top of the legs and at the front and seat of the pants. Take your body measurement with knotted tape and lay this over the pattern pieces on the crotch seam line to assess where the excess length is required— front, back, or both. Use this information to adapt the paper pattern before sewing your pants.

Preparation: Use the knotted tape method, explained on the previous page, and measure your crotch length. Cut out the front and back pants pattern pieces in your size.

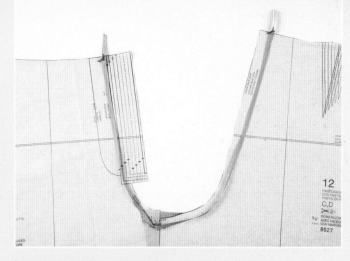

1 Place the pattern pieces together with the knotted tape over the seam lines to compare your own measurements with the pattern. You will see how much of an alteration is required and where the additional length must be placed.

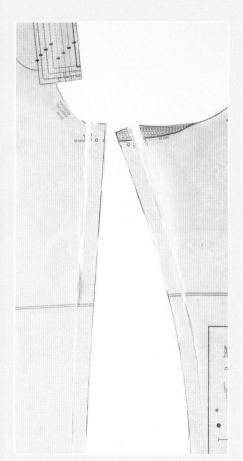

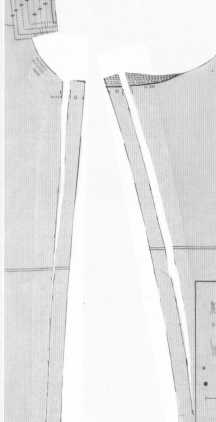

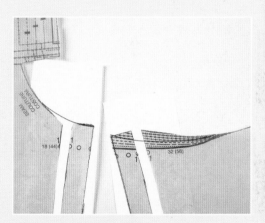

4 Reshape the join in the crotch and smooth off the pattern edge at the knee if necessary, then cut away the excess paper from the pattern.

2 Take the affected pattern piece or pieces and cut along the inside seam allowance from the crotch point to the knee level.

3 Measure on the seam line and move the cut section out to add the necessary length to the seam. The seam allowance section will hinge out from the knee. Tape the pattern to paper placed underneath to hold it in the new position.

Shortening the crotch seam

When the crotch depth on pants is too long, an easy folding adjustment produces a better fit. Check the necessary adjustment required and make a tuck in the paper pattern on the front, back, or both to shorten the crotch depth. This disposes of the excess fabric and gives a closer fit where the crotch depth is short.

Preparation: Use the knotted tape method, explained on page 120, and measure your crotch length. Cut out the front and back pants pattern pieces in your size.

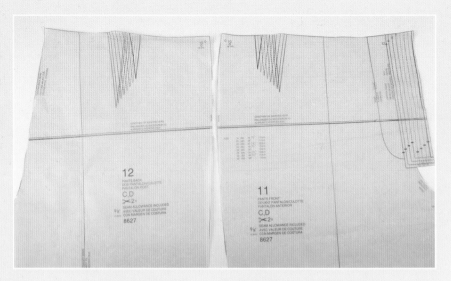

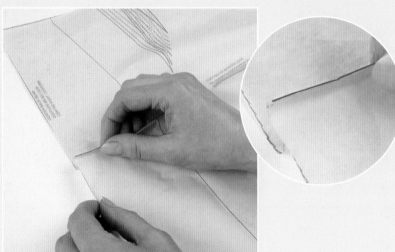

1 Place the front and back pattern pieces together on a flat surface and draw horizontal lines through the hip line or use the lines included on the pattern.

2 Mark the amount to be removed from the crotch seam and make a tuck in the pattern at this point.

3 Take an angled tuck from the crotch seam along the hip line fading to nothing on the side seam. This removes the excess length from the crotch seam but does not affect the outside seam. Glue or tape the fold in place.

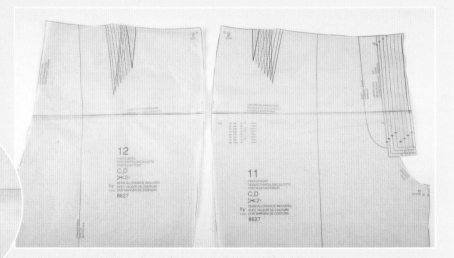

Pants: Bottom

Fitting pants to suit different body shapes can be a challenge because of the complex shape of the pattern. However, working from a standard pattern, adaptations for most figure silhouettes can be achieved. One common figure variation is a large bottom, and additional fullness must be incorporated into the seat of the pattern for a good fit. Unlike a skirt, where the volume is only added to the back of the pattern, pants must also increase the inside leg width under the seat to create ample room for a large bottom.

Pattern adaptation methods

At first sight it may seem appropriate to add to the side and center-back crotch to incorporate the extra fabric required for a large bottom. This would provide more width to span the horizontal circumference, but it does not increase the depth of the seat necessary to improve the fit. Raising the waist level may also seem like a possible option, but this does not introduce the fabric to the correct part of the seat.

To reach the best solution, the back pants pattern piece is cut both vertically and horizontally and spread out to introduce more room in the seat of the pants. The inside leg is also extended to lengthen the crotch seam, since this seam must be longer to travel around. This makes the seat of the pants larger to give room for a full bottom.

If, on the other hand, you have a flat bottom, then you need to slide the cut pattern pieces together, rather than apart. This will remove the excess fullness in the seat of the garment.

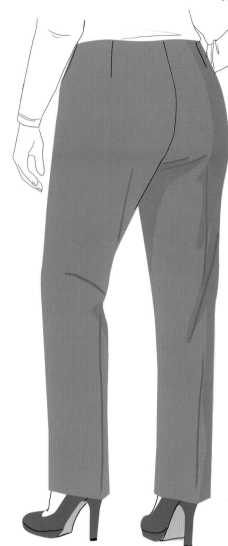

Perfect pants
Alter the pattern for a smooth fit over the bottom and hip.

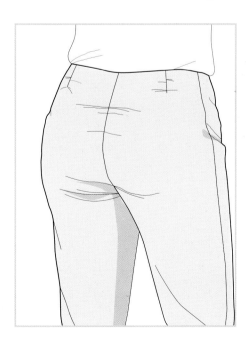

Short seam
Creasing occurs at the side seams and seat where the fabric stretches and pulls to fit. The waistband is pulled downward at the center back because the seam is not long enough to travel comfortably over the rear.

Adapting a pants pattern for a large bottom

Extra fabric must be placed in the correct position at the back of the seat for the best possible fit. Slice the back pattern piece and spread out the parts to add the volume needed and extend the back crotch length on the inside seam.

Preparation: Check the back crotch measurement using the knotted tape method described on page 120. Cut out the back pants pattern in your own size.

1 Compare your measurement with the crotch seam line on the back pattern using either the knotted tape or a tape measure on its side. Calculate the measurement that must be added to the back pattern piece.

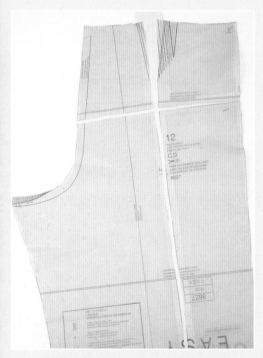

2 Draw a horizontal line across the back, from center back to side seam as shown. Draw a second line, vertically through the center of the leg from the waist dart to the hem. Cut along these lines. Raise the center-back section to add length over the seat and tilt the upper-side piece to the level of the center back. Leave the pattern pieces on the side seam touching to retain the leg length.

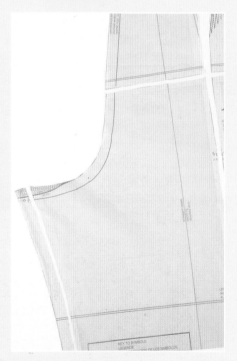

3 Add the final length to the crotch seam by extending the crotch at the inside seam as described on page 121.

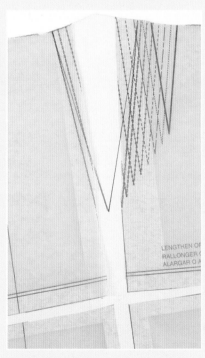

4 Tape the expanded pattern to paper and clean up the pattern edges on the crotch seam and inside leg seam at the knee with smooth lines. Redraw the dart at the waist. It will be wider, but will remain the same length.

Pants: Large stomach

Well-fitting pants are wonderful to wear and look so much better than those that fit poorly. Even with many figure variations, providing we select an appropriate style for our silhouette, pants will look great.

Pattern alteration methods

A large stomach may cause pants to feel tight across the front, showing creases around the bulge. A protruding stomach will also pull on the crotch seam, causing it to rise and giving even more discomfort. These poorly fitted pants will quickly pull out of shape and never look neat, so a pattern alteration before cutting out the fabric is the only solution.

Raising the waist level and moving the side seams out to accommodate a prominent tummy may seem the best approach, but slicing up the paper pattern and moving the pieces apart introduces the fabric directly to the center of the pattern in the area concerned, rather than adding it to the outside edge. The same effect is created, but the shape of the pattern remains, with additional room where it is needed.

Adapting pants for a large stomach is very similar to the adjustment made for a large rear (see page 123–124) but with the changes being made to the front pattern piece instead of the back. As with the prominent bottom, additional length must be introduced to the crotch seam to make the pants fit. This extra length is added to the inside leg on the crotch seam. The pants front is enlarged, too, both across the width and along the length of the front pattern piece.

Large stomach
Creases will appear around the side seams and at top of the legs. The waistband will pull down and apart, straining at the front fastening and zipper, causing the placket to gape. The pants will look and feel uncomfortable.

Adapting pants for a large stomach

Enlarge the front pants pattern for a prominent stomach by opening up the pattern and introducing more fabric to this area. This extends the length of the crotch seam and adds width and length to cover the bulge.

Preparation: Check the front crotch measurement using the knotted tape method described on page 120. Cut out the front pants pattern piece in the appropriate size for your hip and waist.

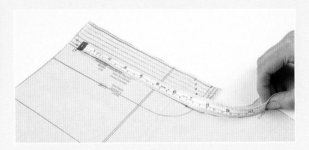

1 Compare your measurement with the crotch seam line on the front pattern either using knotted tape or a tape measure on its side. Follow the seam line and ignore the extension for the zipper placket. Calculate the measurement that must be added for the front crotch to fit.

2 Draw a horizontal line through the pattern from the center front to the side seam on the hip. Draw a second line vertically through the leg from the waist dart to the hem. Cut along these lines to separate the sections.

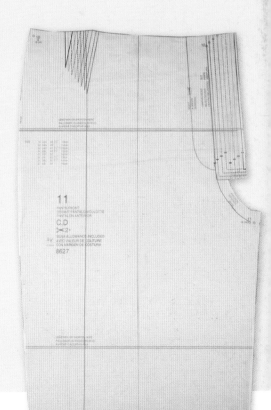

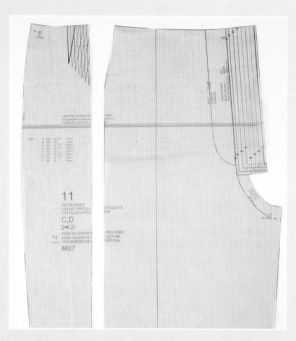

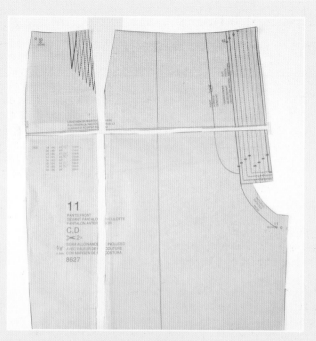

3 Slide the pattern pieces apart to add width across the stomach.

4 Raise the center front to add length over the stomach and tilt the upper-side section to match the level of the center front. Leave the pattern pieces on the side seam touching to retain the leg length.

5 Add the final length to the crotch seam by extending the crotch at the inside seam. Cut through the seam allowance, on the front inside leg, from knee to crotch. Open up the seam allowance to give the additional length needed and taper to the knee.

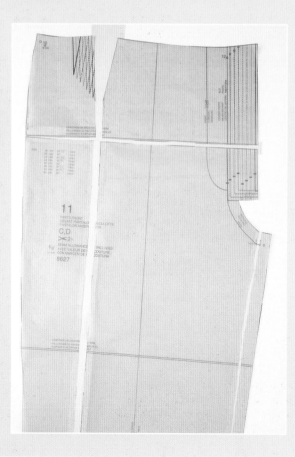

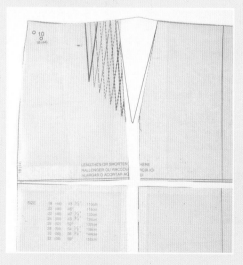

6 Fix the expanded pattern to paper with glue or tape and clean up the pattern edge on the crotch seam. Smooth the inside leg seam at the knee if necessary. Redraw the dart at the waist. If there is a tuck or pleat instead of a dart here, it will be wider to take in the extra fullness at the waist.

Pants: Leg length

The most common alteration required in pants is adapting the length and taking up or dropping the hem to achieve the perfect level. Make small adjustments in hem length when the pants are completed, but for larger amounts it is better to alter the pattern leg length at the start of the process. This retains the line and style of the leg, keeping the proportion in the design.

Leg pattern adjustment methods

To change the leg length in pants at the pattern stage, cut horizontally through the front and back pieces and extend the length or tuck to shorten them as required. Lines are included on paper patterns to indicate where length alterations should be made, but for a very large adjustment in length, choose a second position and split the measurement between the two areas rather than one. This distributes the length better and keeps the leg in proportion for the style.

Choose the right position

Adjusting the length of any pattern piece, whether it is a sleeve, pants leg, or dress involves the same technique. However, the most important factor is choosing the appropriate place to carry out the alteration. An example of this is if you have long legs. Cutting through the top of the pants pattern would extend the crotch depth rather than the leg length. Cutting across the thigh area to open and lengthen the pattern may place the knee level below your own knee position, while extending the pattern in the lower part of the leg may raise the knee position too much. Be aware of your own body structure and alter the pants pattern accordingly. For this reason, lengthening the legs a small amount in two places rather than a larger amount in one is preferable.

Find the perfect hem level

Another issue relating to pants leg length is where the perfect hem level should be in a pair of slacks; too long and the fabric drags on the ground and becomes frayed, but too short and it just looks wrong. When determining the best length for your pants, put on the shoes you plan to wear them with and stand in front of a full-length mirror with a friend to help. Without assistance, every time you look down to check the level, the hem will rise at the back. Pin the hem straight and parallel to the ground then take a good look in the mirror. Use the top of the heel as a guide and assess the length. Raise or lower until the correct length is achieved, then repeat with the other leg.

Leg length is also dependent on style and a narrow leg must be shorter for the shape of the foot, otherwise it will be tight and sit in creases over the shoe. Wider styles can be longer, since they are not restricted by the foot.

X

Long pants
Fabric crumples on top of the shoe and drags on the ground at the back. Correct this at the pattern stage to keep the proportion balanced and improve the length.

X

Short pants
Too much shoe is visible at the front of the foot and above the back of the heel. Unless the pattern is adapted at the start of the process there may not be sufficient hem allowance to correct the short length.

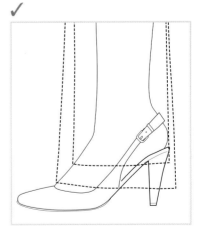

✓

Correct length
The top of the shoe's heel is a good reference point when deciding the appropriate length of pants. However, on very high heels you may prefer to cover more foot by lowering the hem if the style and hem circumference allow it.

Lengthening pants

Getting the perfect pants length is essential and this is best carried out at the pattern stage, especially if a large adjustment must be made. Take your leg measurement from the waist, over the hip to the required level at the hem, and compare this with the information given on the pattern. If you need to lengthen your pants, this difference indicates the amount necessary.

Preparation: Calculate the measurement to be added to the leg length and cut out the front and back pattern pieces in the appropriate size.

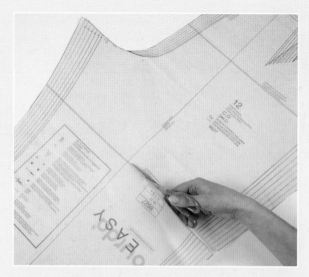

1 Cut the pattern pieces along the length adjustment lines of the pattern on both back and front.

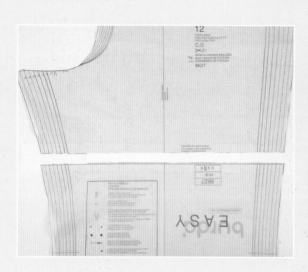

2 Spread the pattern pieces apart by the amount needed, keeping the grain line straight. Place paper below and fix in place. Make sure the front and back pieces are treated the same.

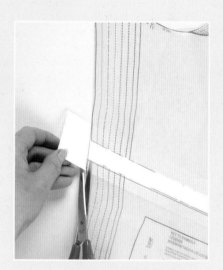

3 Smooth the edges of the joins to straighten the seam lines and trim away excess paper. The pattern is now ready to cut out in fabric.

Shortening pants

In the same way that the pant legs were extended to add length, make folds along the same lines to shorten the pants.

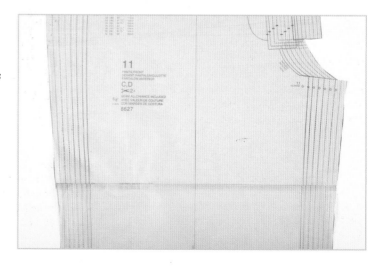

Dresses: Length, proportion, and fit

Getting a dress to fit well is not quite as simple as fitting separates, because back length and leg length play such an important part in the proportion of the figure. If you have a long back and relatively short legs, you can make a standard-sized skirt and top fit without much adjustment. A dress, on the other hand, is not likely to sit in the correct position at the waist, so some alteration is necessary to improve the proportion.

Dress proportion adjustments

As with most clothing alterations, a perfect fit can be achieved at the toile stage when the fabric can be pinned accurately to the curves and contours of the body (see page 136). However, the proportion and length of a dress can be modified at the pattern stage so that only fine-tuning needs to be carried out when the toile is fitted. Where there is no waist seam on a dress, for example, on a princess-seam style, it is more difficult to make adjustments while the dress is being constructed, so a modification at the pattern stage is essential.

Having accurate nape-to-waist and waist-to-hip measurements is key to achieving a good fit when making a dress. The main measurements of a finished garment are normally stated on the back of the pattern envelope so that you can compare these with your own. This will indicate where you may need to adapt the pattern.

A dress with no waist seam will require length adjustments at the start so that the bust, waist, and hip levels match your own when it is sewn.

Dress fitting adjustments

Having corrected the proportion of the dress so that the bust, waist, and hip levels are right, you may also need to alter for a hollow back to avoid excess fullness between the waist and hip at the back. Because there is no horizontal seam to make adjustments later, it is wise to adapt the pattern before cutting out the fabric. Where there is a waist seam, any adjustments must be made to the waist of both bodice and skirt pattern pieces.

Perfectly proportioned dress
Modify a dress pattern so that the bust, waist, and hip are in the appropriate positions.

Poor dress proportion
When a dress does not match the figure, the bust, waist, and hip levels are not in the same position as the body. This results in wrinkles and creasing where there is excess cloth and pulling in the areas where the dress is tight.

Hollow back in a dress
When there is no waist seam to alter a dress for a hollow back, the pattern must be adjusted before cutting out, otherwise wrinkling appears at the small of the back between the waist and hip.

Adapting dress proportion (no waist seam)

For a dress to fit well, the bust, waist, and hip levels must match your own. Measure from your nape to waist, shoulder to bust, and waist to hip, and compare these with the actual pattern. If a length adjustment is required, transfer this information to the pattern and extend or fold where necessary to achieve the correct figure proportion.

Preparation: Take your body measurements and cut out all the main pattern pieces for your dress in the appropriate size.

1 Lay out the pattern pieces side by side and draw lines across the pattern in the places where an alteration is needed.

2 Cut and move the pattern sections apart to add length and fold the pattern to shorten the length. Keep the grain lines level to ensure the pattern does not become twisted, and redraw the darts. Apply the same adjustments to all the pattern pieces.

3 Repeat these changes on any facings to ensure they match when the garment is sewn together.

burda

Adapting a hollow back on a dress without a waist seam

If adapting a dress with a waist seam to fit a figure silhouette with a hollow back, follow the instructions on page 104. This explains how to adapt the back waist of a skirt and it can be attached to the bodice to give a good fit. On a dress with no horizontal seam, the dress pattern is altered in a slightly different way.

Preparation: Cut out the dress pattern in an appropriate size and have the back piece or pieces ready to alter.

1 If there are multiple back pattern pieces, pin these together along the seams. Use pins with small heads to avoid distorting the seam.

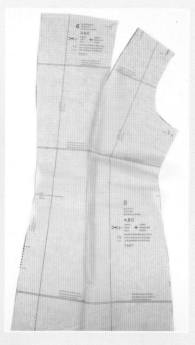

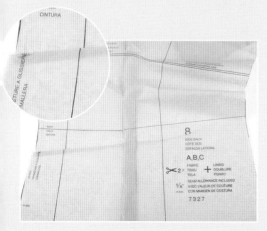

2 Locate the waist and draw it on the pattern. Mark a point below the waist—at the center back—for the length reduction sufficient for the hollow back.

3 Make a fold joining the two points at the center back and angle this to the side seam. This removes the length at the back waist but leaves the side seam the same length. Secure with tape to hold the modification.

4 Take out the pins and separate the pattern pieces. The side back is ready to cut in fabric, but redraw the grain line on the center back, continuing the direction from the lower part of the arrow. The upper-center back is now slightly off-grain.

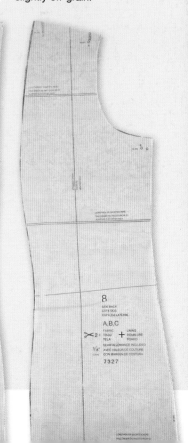

Dresses: Using multi-size patterns

Our figure variations mean that we do not always fit the standard patterns available to us. However, that does not mean that we have to put up with a poor fit. One of the best ways to achieve a well-fitting dress is to use a multi-size pattern that offers a large range of sizes inside one envelope.

The benefits of multi-size dress patterns

Such patterns are ideal when waists, hips, and busts are not quite in proportion, and you can use the appropriate size lines where they are needed. If you are a classic pear shape, for example, you will have a narrow waist in comparison to your hip measurement, so you can choose different pattern lines to follow for your hip and waist when cutting out a skirt or dress. Where the two areas meet, a neat new line is drawn to join the figure parts so that the finished skirt or dress matches your silhouette perfectly.

Without a multi-size pattern, you would need to buy a pattern that suits only part of your figure and make alterations to fit the rest of your body. Alternatively, a more expensive option is to buy more than one pattern to make a well-fitting outfit. This is especially relevant when making one-piece dresses or tunics that cover the bust, waist, and hip.

You can, of course, use a one-size pattern and make alterations at the toile stage if you choose to (see page 136). However, if you range over a number of sizes (for example, 22 bodice and 18 hip) the dress toile may be far too big, or worse, too small, to make pinning the amended shape easy or even possible. A much better approach is to use a multi-size pattern and highlight the appropriate size lines, joining them where necessary before cutting out the fabric and sewing up your dress. Fine-tuning can always be done on the toile but by using a pattern with multiple sizes, a closer fit is likely to be achieved with only minor alterations necessary.

Well-fitting dress
Multi-size patterns make it easier to achieve a perfect fit.

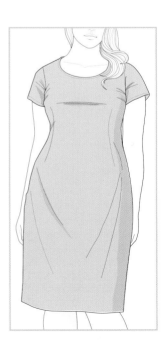

Poorly fitting dress
Without the help of a multi-size pattern, it is more difficult to get a good fit when making a dress. It will mean fitting one part of the figure—for example, the bodice or hip—and enlarging or shrinking the rest of the dress to fit. Without an alteration, some parts of the dress will be too loose or tight rather than giving an elegant overall fit.

Adapting a multi-size dress pattern

Use a multi-size pattern to create a garment to fit your personal body shape by selecting the appropriate size lines. The secret of success is to merge the size lines naturally to give a smooth outline that follows your figure contours. Armed with accurate figure measurements, you can compare these with the standard chart given in the pattern and work out which sizes are relevant for you. You will need to know the best size in which to cut out your bodice pieces, as well as the waist and hip appropriate for you.

Preparation: Take accurate figure measurements and compare your measurements with the size chart inside the pattern, and decide which pattern sizes you cover. Gather together the relevant pattern pieces, including the facings, to create your dress.

1 Iron the paper pattern, without steam, to remove all the creases and to make it easier to work with. Any creases left in the pattern may lead to inaccuracies.

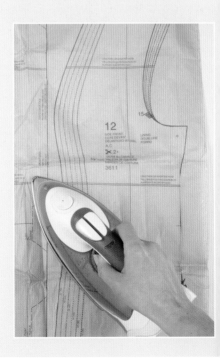

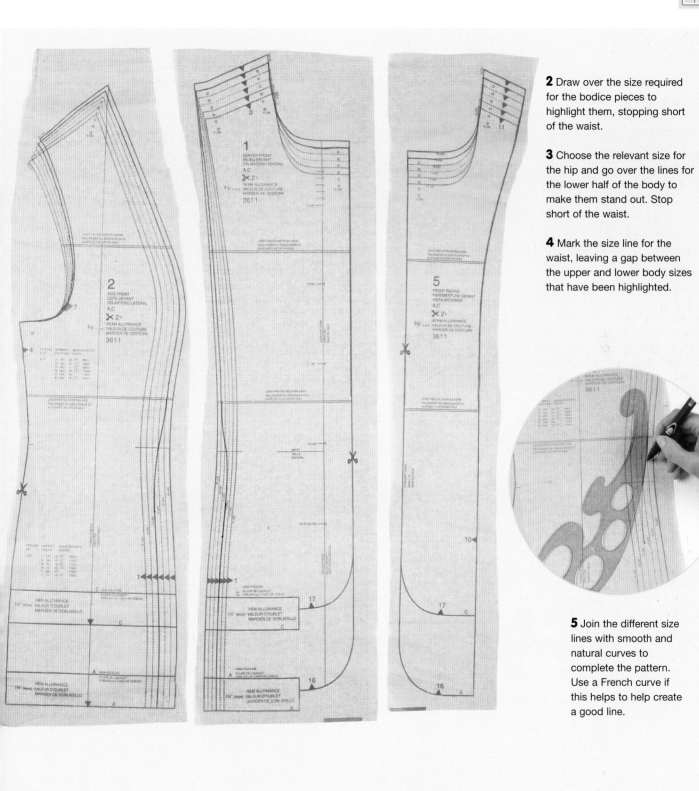

2 Draw over the size required for the bodice pieces to highlight them, stopping short of the waist.

3 Choose the relevant size for the hip and go over the lines for the lower half of the body to make them stand out. Stop short of the waist.

4 Mark the size line for the waist, leaving a gap between the upper and lower body sizes that have been highlighted.

5 Join the different size lines with smooth and natural curves to complete the pattern. Use a French curve if this helps to help create a good line.

Making a toile

This section details the process of making and altering a toile to achieve a perfect fit before transferring the information back onto the paper pattern. The principles described may also be used to improve the fit of ready-made clothing.

Making a toile

People make their own clothes for a variety of reasons—perhaps to wear something unique or with an exceptional finish on the inside, not always evident in store-bought clothing. One major reason people choose to sew their own garments at home is to get a flattering and comfortable fit. With all our many shapes and sizes, it is easier to do this by sewing our own fashions than buying a standard size off the rack.

Finding the perfect fit

When home sewing, the way to achieve that perfect fit is by planning ahead and taking the stages one step at a time. First, take accurate measurements and from these select the most appropriate size(s) to use. Next, make any adjustments to the pattern to improve the overall fit. This may mean altering the length of the pieces to suit your height or modifications for particular features such as sloping shoulders or a hollow back. Having altered the paper pattern, cut out the pieces in muslin fabric and make a test garment, or toile. This can be fitted on the body and pinned and adjusted until a perfect fit is reached. Any adjustments made at this stage can be transferred back onto the paper pattern so that it can be used for the final garment with the confidence of knowing it will fit well. One final tip for a pattern that is likely to be used over and over again is to back it with a medium-weight fusible interfacing to lengthen the life of the pattern. You can then make the same garment many times in different fabrics.

Use a toile for all types of garment, whether skirts, blouses, dresses, or pants. Although it takes longer to complete a piece of clothing if you go through all these stages, you will know that it will fit you perfectly and will avoid wasted hours of sewing, and the prospect of dealing with an alteration at the end.

What is a toile?

A toile is a test garment or prototype made up to check the fit and style. Muslin is a stable, inexpensive cloth and was traditionally used for toile making because it does not pull out of shape and you can see how it lies over the figure. The exception to this is when making a garment in stretch fabric, in which case use a fabric with a similar weight and degree of stretch to the fashion cloth. When the toile is created and put on, any necessary adjustments will be obvious; loose fabric can be pinned away or seams opened up to allow more room. Muslin is light in color and balance points and lines can be marked onto it to see where it does or does not follow the contours of your body. At this stage, facings, fastenings, and edge finishes are not included, allowing easy access and adjustment to all parts of the toile.

Ideally, you need a good friend to help at this stage and a large mirror to spot any problems. If the garment is for a special occasion, wear the undergarments you plan to wear with it and the correct shoes to gauge the finished length. If this is not possible, invest in an adjustable tailor's dummy or dress form. To make it more like your own body, set it to your personal measurements and pad out any areas needed to reflect your shape. This can be covered with a layer of stockinette, or you can buy specially designed dress-form covers to smooth over the surface.

The fitting process

Follow these stages to achieve a perfectly fitted garment.

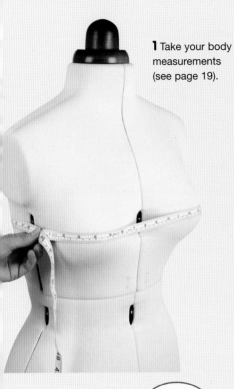

1 Take your body measurements (see page 19).

4 Make a toile and fine-tune the fit (see page 136).

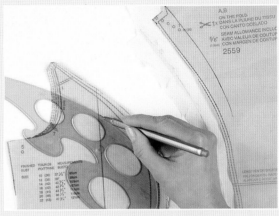

5 Transfer the changes to the pattern (see pages 140–152).

2 Select the appropriate pattern size (see page 40).

3 Adjust for length and specific figure variations (see pages 50–133).

6 Make up pattern in fashion fabric (see pages 156–173 for core techniques).

Creating your toile

Create your toile as you would any other garment, paying special attention to keeping accurate seam allowances to make sure the completed prototype is as close to perfect as possible. Iron out any creases from the muslin fabric before you start and follow the grain lines precisely. Drawing the bust, waist, and hip lines on the fabric and any other relevant markings is helpful so that they can be compared with your own body. Sew up the seams, leaving a gap for the zipper or fastening, but mark the seam line and button and buttonhole positions so that the toile can be pinned correctly in place when you put it on.

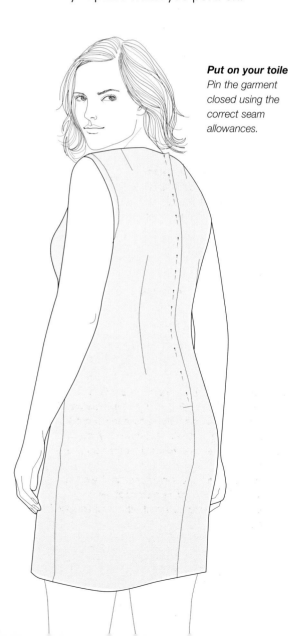

Put on your toile
Pin the garment closed using the correct seam allowances.

Fitting your toile
When your toile is created and ready to put on, get someone to pin you into it or place it on your dress form and close the gaps with pins. Run through the following points to assess how well your toile fits your figure. Look at all aspects of the fit before making any adjustments. Use the same order to make your changes unless one area in particular catches your attention.

Getting started
Get an overall view of the fit and make a mental note of where the toile is tight or loose over your body and therefore where attention will be required.

Waist
Tie a length of elastic lightly around your waist to see if this lies naturally at the waist of the toile. If it does not, mark the true waist on the toile to show whether it should be raised or lowered. To raise the toile waist, make a tuck above it to pinch out the extra length. To lower it, measure the distance from toile waist to the elastic and transfer this additional length to the bodice pattern.

If the size of the waist of the toile does not match your own, reshape the seams and/or darts, sharing the excess or shortage between them. Either pin the seams and darts in or unpick the stitches and repin them on a new line.

Bust
Compare your own bust level and the bust points, or apex, with the toile. One way to check the bust line of the toile against your own is to place masking tape over your

underwear at bust level before putting it on. If they do not match up, mark your own bust level and apex on the toile. If the bust level is too high or too low, measure the distance so that the pattern can be shortened or lengthened to suit. If the bust points are too far apart or too close together, a vertical adjustment should be made by making a tuck or slicing and opening the pattern to move the apex to the correct position.

The position of the darts in relation to the bust points should be considered. The point of the dart should be angled toward the bust point but stop short of it; the larger the bust, the farther away the dart point should be. Providing your bust level and the bust line of the toile are the same, you should only need to adjust the dart length.

Sleeves

Check whether the sleeve sits naturally in the armhole at the shoulder and rotate to improve the way it hangs if necessary. Compare your elbow level with the sleeve and make a note of how much to adjust the sleeve to level them up. Having corrected the elbow level, make width adjustments if the upper arm is tight in the sleeve and finally, check the length. Pin up the hem allowance and mark any changes from this level.

Neckline

Look for tightness or gaping around the neck both at the front and in the back. Pin any adjustments necessary, which can be transferred to the pattern.

Shoulders

Look at your shoulder from the side and check that the toile is lying naturally. If there is excess fabric on the shoulder, the angle may need to be changed. Pin along the seam to remove the surplus fabric.

If the shoulders roll forward, mark the toile where pattern adjustments are needed to improve the fit.

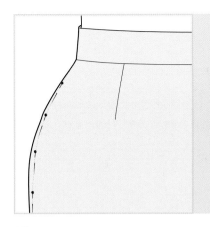

Hip contour

Pin the excess fabric to reshape the hip silhouette to match your figure.

Hip

If your hip level and the hip line marked on the toile are not in the same place, measure the difference. Adjust this by making a tuck in the toile to level them up or transfer this information to the pattern to lengthen the distance from waist to hip.

The contour of your hip may be quite different to the toile. Pin any excess to match the hip shape or unpick the stitches and let out the side seams as required.

Consider the length of the waist darts in the assessment of your hip, too. A very long dart may make the skirt or pants ride up.

Finished length

When all other alterations have been made, consider the finished length and pin the hem up parallel to the floor. When correct, mark the new hemline on the toile and adjust the position on the pattern using the original hem allowance depth.

To finish

Transfer all adjustments to the pattern, and if necessary, make a second toile to confirm that the adjustments have been made appropriately.

Tips for toile making

- Press out any creases in the muslin fabric with a hot iron before you start.
- Be precise when working. This includes marking and cutting out the pattern as well as when cutting the muslin. Make sure notches are cut in the correct places.
- Mark the important details directly onto the toile, including the center front, dart positions, and bust, waist, and hip levels. Transfer the apex or bust points to the toile.
- Transfer all the pattern markings consistently to the right side of the fabric. This makes it simpler to recognize the right and wrong sides

and makes it easier to pin adjustments when on the dress form.
- Lengthen the stitch to approximately 8 spi (3 mm) when sewing the toile. This is still short enough to hold the seams together but it makes unpicking easier if necessary when adjusting the fit.
- Use an accurate ⅝ in (1.5 cm) seam allowance for the seams and follow dart positions carefully.
- When the toile is constructed, iron the seams open and snip and notch for a flat finish. This helps with the accuracy of the fit.
- Label the toile with the date and size so that it will not be confused with subsequent prototypes.

Toile fitting: Princess seams

Choosing a princess-style pattern is an excellent way to achieve a good fit because the position of the seams makes it easy to make adjustments to follow the shape of the figure. Create the toile using the guidelines on pages 136–139 and check the fit.

Princess-seam dress—too large

Here, a princess seam has been used that travels the length of the dress and curves through the bust to the armhole. Any changes are made at the seam to help the dress to fit more closely to the upper body.

1 Where there is extra material in the toile, pin the muslin over the seam to pinch out the surplus.

2 Mark the line of pins on both sides of the seam to show the new shape of the seam where you have altered it.

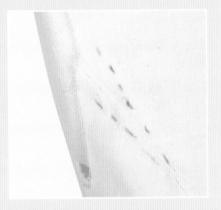

3 Take out the pins, unpick the seam, then press the toile pieces flat.

4 Trace the line to create a natural seam line. Do this by hand or with the help of a French curve.

5 Place the paper pattern over the toile and match up the seams and edges. Trace the newly shaped line from the toile below.

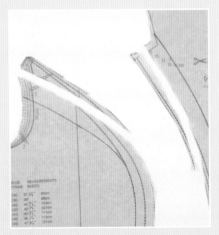

6 Trim the outside edge—the cutting line—making it ⅝ in (1.5 cm) from the altered seam line.

Princess-seam dress—too small

In this example, the princess-style design features vertical seams that run through the bust to the shoulder rather than the armhole. Although different to the previous example, it is still a princess-style dress.

1 Examine the fit of the toile on the figure or dress form and look for areas where it is too tight.

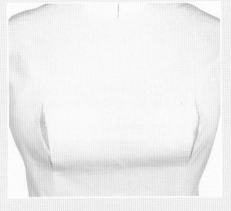

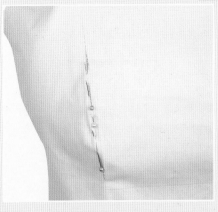

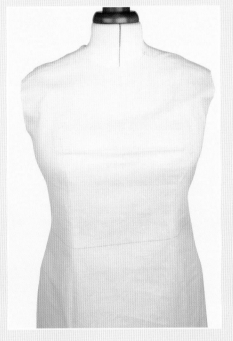

2 Where the toile is tight over the bust area, unpick the seam to release the stitching to allow the side seams to sit in the correct position.

3 Pin the seam back together following a new line on the seam allowance and joining with the existing seam at each end. Form a smooth seam.

4 Mark the new seam line with a pencil on both sides of the seam.

5 Remove the toile from the dress form, unpick the seams, then iron the toile panels flat. Redraw a smooth seam line using the marks as a guide.

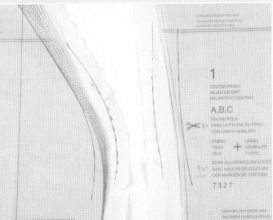

7 Add paper to the outside edge of the pattern and draw the cutting line ⅝ in (1.5 cm) outside the seam line. Trim away the excess to produce the newly shaped pattern pieces.

6 Place the paper pattern over the toile and match up the seams and edges. Trace the newly shaped line from the toile below.

Toile fitting: Waist and bust darts

While a princess style offers the best opportunity to adjust a dress to give a really close fit, a garment with darts allows adjustment at this point. If there are both waist and bust darts, it is easy to add fabric or remove it where necessary, but where there are only waist darts, more manipulation is needed to get the shaping required. If there is a big surplus of fabric at the armhole or bust, an extra dart can be formed but a smaller amount can be repositioned into the waist dart by adapting the toile and pattern.

Waist dart in bodice—adding a bust dart

Where there is excess fabric in the bodice of a dress or blouse, it can be removed by creating a bust dart to improve the shape and fit. Simply make up the toile and pin away the fabric in the gaping area and control it with a dart.

1 Put on the toile and pinch out the excess fabric along the most appropriate line.

2 Draw along the pin line with a pencil on both sides of the pinned-out fabric to show how much must be removed.

3 Remove the toile, unpick the seams, separate the dress panels, then iron the toile flat. Use the marks as a guide and draw the new dart in place.

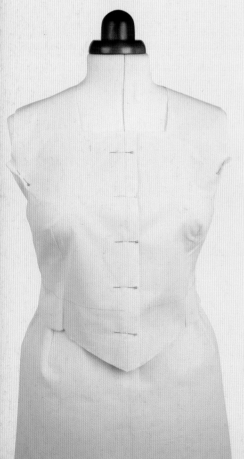

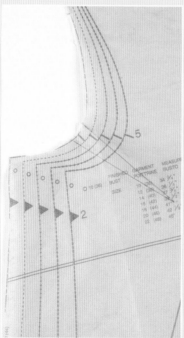

4 Place the toile beneath the paper pattern and transfer the new dart onto the pattern.

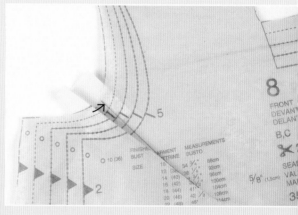

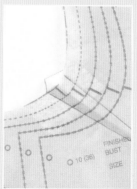

5 Tape paper to the edge of the pattern and close up the dart, folding it downward as it will lie when sewn. Follow the armhole outline to correct the shape of the pattern edge.

6 Trim along the reshaped armhole and open up the dart.

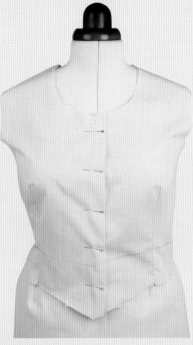

Waist dart in bodice—gaping armhole

Where there is excess fabric in the dress front, it can be redistributed into the existing waist dart by pinning away and manipulating the excess.

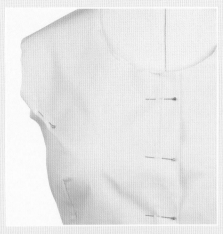

1 Create the toile, put it on, and pin it in place. Check for loose fabric.

2 Pinch out the excess muslin with pins in the area to give a smooth line from the bust.

3 Mark the pin line with a pencil on both sides of the fabric, then remove the pins.

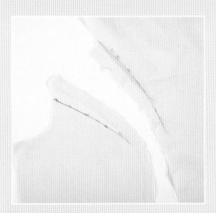

4 Take off the toile and remove the stitches from the original dart.

5 Cut through the original dart in the toile.

6 Close up the new dart drawn on the toile. This will open up the original dart further.

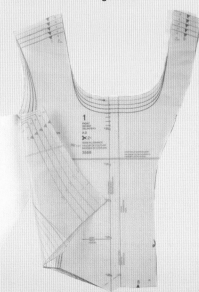

7 Place the pattern over the toile, using pins to hold the layers together securely. Draw in the wider waist dart and redraw the waistline edge if necessary.

Toile fitting: Armholes

It is important that a garment fits well where the sleeve meets the armhole, both for comfort and for a good appearance. If it is too loose, the jacket or dress appears too big, and if it is too small the fabric will pull and appear tight under the arm.

Jacket—too big

Where there is too much fabric at the bust level of a jacket, it must be made smaller. This means the sleeve width must also be reduced so that it fits neatly into the armhole.

1 Pin the sleeve out of the way so that you can see where you are working. Pin out the excess fabric in the side seams to improve the fit.

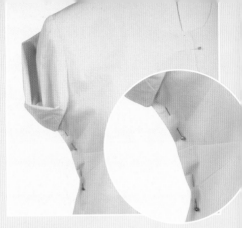

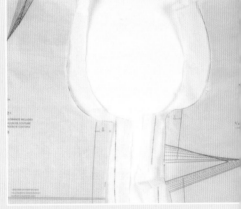

4 Remove the toile from the dress form, unpick the seams to separate the panels, and iron the pieces flat.

5 Lay the bodice front and back toile panels on a work surface and cover with the pattern pieces. Trace the new seam lines onto the pattern.

Jacket—too small

If a jacket is too tight and requires a side-seam alteration, the sleeve must be adjusted to match so the pieces continue to fit together at the armhole.

1 Unpick the lower half of the sleeve from the armhole and undo the stitches of the side seam as far as required.

2 Repin the side seam to fit and mark with a pen or pencil.

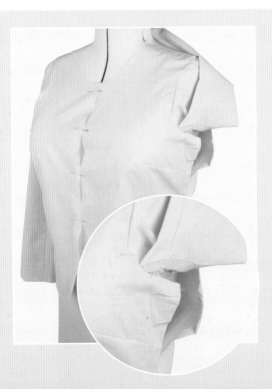

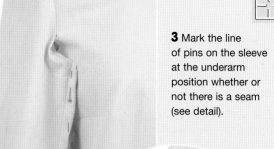

2 Unpick the lower half of the sleeve from the armhole and pin the sleeve the same amount as the side seam at the underarm. This may be at a seam or in the middle of a panel, depending on the sleeve style.

3 Mark the line of pins on the sleeve at the underarm position whether or not there is a seam (see detail).

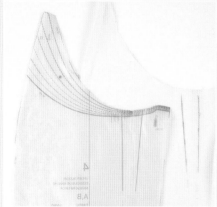

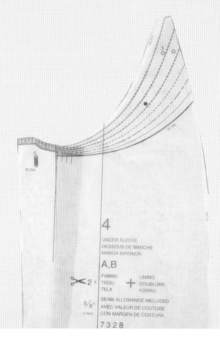

6 Place the sleeve or part-sleeve toile flat on the work surface and cover with the pattern. Transfer the markings from the toile to the pattern.

7 Reshape the sleeve piece with a tuck if the sleeve is in two pieces or adjust the seam lines if the style has a one-piece sleeve.

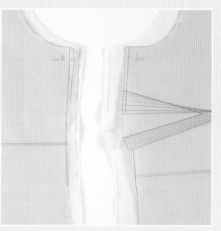

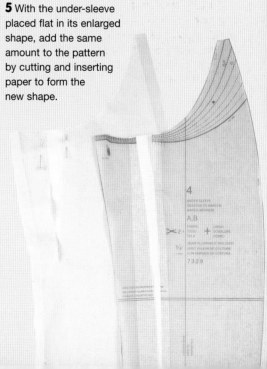

5 With the under-sleeve placed flat in its enlarged shape, add the same amount to the pattern by cutting and inserting paper to form the new shape.

3 Unpick the sleeve seam if there is a one-piece sleeve or cut through the panel if the sleeve is made up of two parts. Add a piece of fabric and pin the gap open to the correct enlargement.

4 Remove the toile from the dress form and unpick the seams to separate the panels. Place the front and back toile pieces flat on a work surface and cover with the pattern pieces. Transfer the new seam lines to the pattern.

Toile fitting: Back, neck, and shoulders

It is important that the back, shoulders, and neckline fit well and sit flat without gaping or creasing. Various features may prevent a smooth fit here, so take time to assess where the problem stems from. Unpick or repin the seams to allow a flat finish and to establish the alteration required.

Note: In this example, the yoke and back pattern pieces were pinned along the seam before being placed over the toile, then the center-back line was marked through both.

Center back

The center-back seam, which may include a zipper, can be altered to match the shape of the figure. Try on the toile and mark the line necessary for a good fit.

1 Pin the center-back folds together on the seam line to check the fit, then repin following the shape of the back.

Neckline

When a neckline gapes or is too tight, adjust the shoulder seams to achieve a smoother finish.

1 Unpick or adjust the shoulder seam with pins to achieve a smooth neckline, removing any crinkles or pulling.

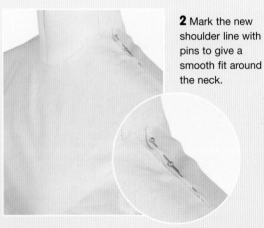

2 Mark the new shoulder line with pins to give a smooth fit around the neck.

3 Mark the adjusted shoulder seam and redraw the neckline if necessary.

4 Separate the toile parts and press the toile flat. Draw the revised shoulder seam.

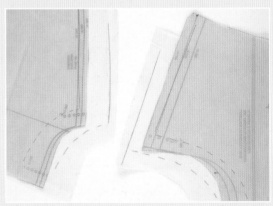

5 Transfer the new shoulder line and neckline to the pattern. Trim or add paper to provide an accurate ⅝ in (1.5 cm) seam allowance.

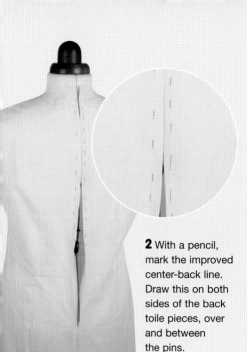

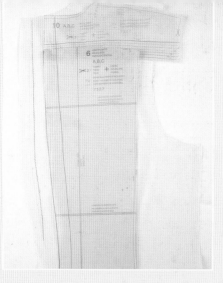

2 With a pencil, mark the improved center-back line. Draw this on both sides of the back toile pieces, over and between the pins.

3 Remove the pins and press the pieces flat. Working with uncreased muslin and tissue makes the changes more accurate. Draw in a smooth center-back line using the marks as a guide.

4 Place the back pattern piece over the toile and transfer the new line to the paper pattern to form a natural curve for the center-back seam.

Shoulder width

Having to adjust the shoulder length of a garment is very common and relatively easy to do.

1 Take a look at the head of the shoulder and see whether it sits on the shoulder bone. Here, the sleeve collapses because the shoulder seam is too long.

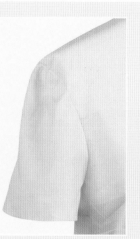

2 Pin a new line along the shoulder seam, working from the correct position at the head of the sleeve. Smooth the line into the curve of the armhole. Mark with a pen or pencil.

3 Unpick the sleeve from the armhole and lift the sleeve into the new position to confirm whether it is correct.

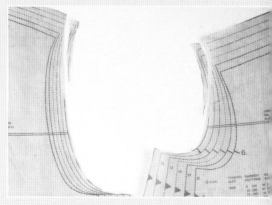

4 Remove the toile from the dress form and separate the pieces, then iron them flat. Mark the new sewing line on the toile.

5 Mark a line ⅝ in (1.5 cm) from the new armhole line for the seam allowance.

6 Transfer the new armhole shaping to the paper pattern and trim away the excess (or add if extending the shoulder seam).

Toile fitting: Hip and waist shaping

Creating a good fit at the waist and hip of a garment is relatively simple, since adjustments can be made at the seams and darts to achieve the correct contouring. Remove excess material by taking in seams and darts, or let them out to create more room in a garment. Put on the toile and adjust as required.

Loose fit

If a skirt is too large at the waist, it will shift and drop below the waist. Reshape the seams so that it will sit at the correct level.

1 Close up the zipper position on the back with pins along the seam line.

2 Lift the skirt up into the correct position and place pins at the side seams of the waist to hold it in place.

4 With a line of pins, follow the side seam over the hip to the hem, running parallel to the side seam from below the widest part of the hip.

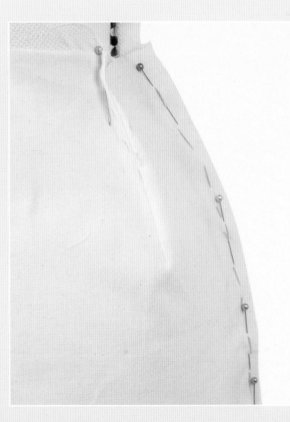

5 Mark at and between the pin positions on both side seams to show the new, better-fitting side seam.

3 Check the darts and pin these in further if required. If not, carry out all adjustments at the side seams.

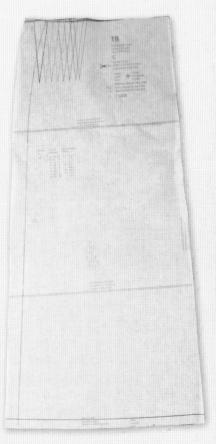

6 Open the seams and press flat, then true the side seam. Place the paper pattern over the marked toile and trace through the new seam line position.

7 Mark the changes on both back and front pattern pieces. Make sure the two seams reflect the same outline.

Tight fit

A tight-fitting skirt is uncomfortable to wear. Adjust the toile as follows and transfer the adjustments back onto the pattern for an improved fit.

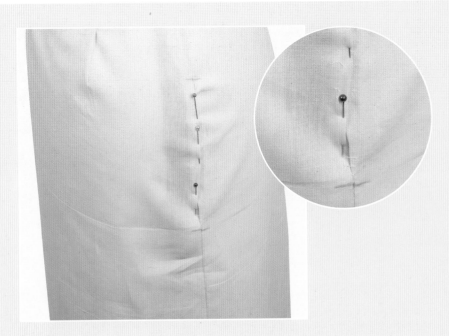

1 Release the seam where it is too tight across the hip, repin, and mark a new line on the seam allowance. This may be a short length or the entire seam. If there is not enough seam allowance to adjust the toile, sew the toile in a larger size.

2 Remove the pins and separate the pieces, then iron them flat. Draw in the revised side seam.

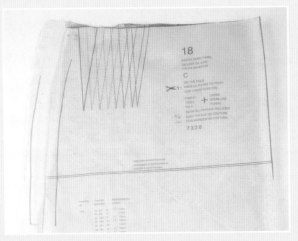

3 Position the pattern over the toile and trace the new seam lines.

4 Add paper to the pattern edges and include a ⅝ in (1.5 cm) seam allowance, then trim away the extra paper.

Dart length

Getting the correct dart length is vital to creating a smooth silhouette at the waist. A simple dart adjustment can make a great deal of difference.

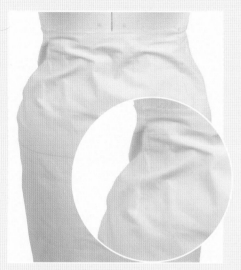

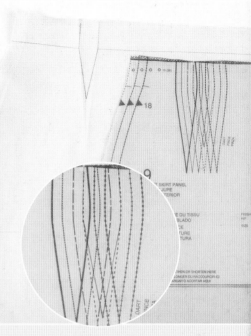

1 When the darts are too long for the curve of the figure, a skirt tends to ride up, with excess fabric bunching at the waist.

2 Unpick the darts and repin them to a shorter length, allowing the skirt to sit on the hip comfortably.

3 Remove the toile from the dress form and true the lines of the dart. Transfer the new darts to the paper pattern.

Dart position

If the waist darts on a skirt are too far apart, they can make the stomach appear larger than it really is.

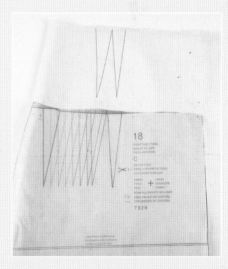

1 Mark the dart positions but do not sew them.

2 Pin the darts in the preferred position and to the correct length to suit your figure.

3 Mark the new darts on the toile and transfer this to the paper pattern pieces.

Smoothing a hollow back

A hollow back often causes a skirt or dress to bunch up with excess fabric at the small of the back. Use the toile to determine how much fabric must be removed for a smooth finish, then transfer the alteration to the paper pattern.

  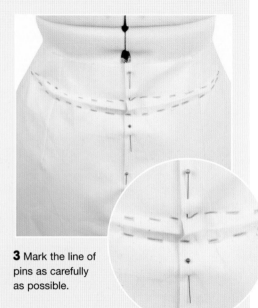

1 Sew the toile and press the seams flat. Put it on the dress form, pinning up the zipper position.

2 There will be excess fabric at the lower back. Pin this away in a straight line from the center back to the side seam.

3 Mark the line of pins as carefully as possible.

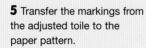 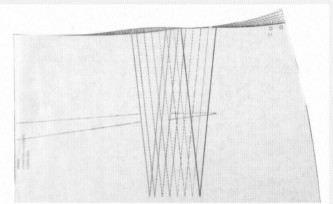

4 Remove the toile from the dress form and separate the pieces. Iron out the seam line creases.

5 Transfer the markings from the adjusted toile to the paper pattern.

6 Make a tuck to remove the extra length from the center back. Adjust the lines of the back dart and straighten the center-back seam.

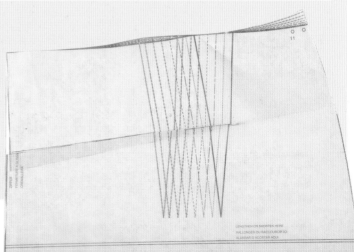

Toile fitting: Hem leveling

The final step to checking your prototype garment is to create a level hem in a suitable length.

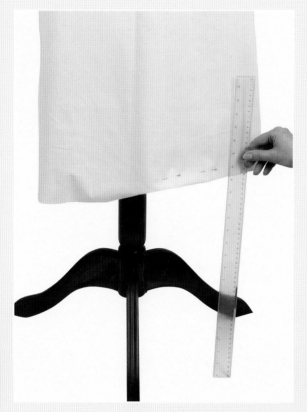

Leveling the hem

There are specialist gadgets available for marking hems, but a long ruler or yardstick is sufficient.

1 Pin the skirt in place and put on the shoes that will be worn with the outfit, unless using a dress form. Decide on the length required and pin a small area of the hem to check. If correct, measure the distance from the floor.

2 Take out the pins and place one pin at the level required.

3 Work carefully around the hem, placing a pin at the same level around the circumference.

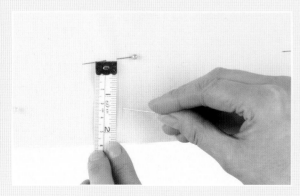

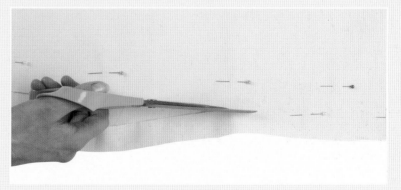

4 Decide on the depth of hem (e.g ⅝ in/1.5 cm; 1¼ in/3 cm; 3 in/7.5 cm) and mark this distance below the pin level. Use a line of pins or a fabric-marking pen to do so.

5 Cut away the surplus fabric and shorten the hem with your choice of method (see pages 160–161). Transfer the new skirt length to the paper pattern.

Core techniques

Use this section for reference when sewing your perfectly fitting garments. It includes the basic sewing and construction techniques with step-by-step illustrations to make them easy to follow.

Seams

Seams join pieces of fabric together. Your choice of seam will depend on the fabric being used, the purpose of the piece of clothing, and where the seam lies within it. Use the advice provided to help you choose appropriately.

Helpful hints

- Always secure the start and end of every seam with a reverse stitch to prevent the seam from unraveling.
- Press the stitches of a seam with an iron before opening the seam up. This helps to give a smooth, wrinkle-free finish.
- Cut off thread ends as you sew. Leaving them may create unnecessary tangles and could be time-consuming if left until the end of the project.
- Choose sewing-machine needles appropriately when sewing, considering both size and type. This will prevent skipped stitches and damage to delicate fabrics.

Plain seam

This is the simplest way to join two pieces of fabric together and is suitable for all weights and types of fabric. Use this method for straight and curved seams.

1 Place the right sides of the fabric together and pin along the sewing line ⅝ in (1.5 cm) from the edge.

2 Set the sewing machine for straight stitching and sew along the seam line, removing the pins in the process.

3 When completed, press the seam open and finish the raw edges.

Flat-fell seam

The seam allowance on a flat-fell seam is tucked under and topstitched. Use it for reversible garments and for a flat finish, since the raw edges are completely enclosed. It is often used for jeans and denim clothing.

1 With the wrong sides of the fabric together, pin and sew a line of straight stitching on the seam line.

2 Press the seam allowances to one side and trim the under-edge to ⅛ in (3 mm).

3 Tuck the outside ¼ in (6 mm) of the upper seam allowance under and pin to the fabric below, covering the trimmed edge of the other seam allowance.

4 Edge stitch, on the fold, securing the seam to the layers below.

French seam

A French seam looks like a plain seam from the right side with a tuck enclosing the raw edges, and pressed to one side on the reverse. This makes a delicate seam perfect for light- and medium-weight fabrics.

 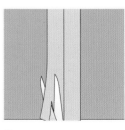 

1 With the wrong sides of the fabric together and edges level, machine a line of stitching ¼ in (6 mm) from the edge.

2 Press the seam open and trim the raw edges to approximately ⅛ in (3 mm).

3 Fold the seam so that the right sides are now together and enclosing the trimmed edges. Pin and stitch ¼ in (6 mm) from the folded edge.

Boned seam

For bridal and evening wear, a boned seam is a good way to provide internal support for a bodice and to allow it to hold itself up. Casings must be created at the seams for the bones to slide into.

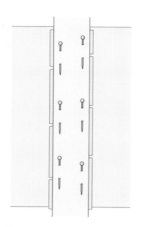

1 Sew a plain seam and press open. If the seam is curved, snip the edges of the seam allowance so the seam lies smoothly.

2 Place a length of ¾-in (2-cm) wide satin bias ribbon face down over the wrong side of the seam and pin the edges to the seam allowance.

3 Edge stitch through the ribbon and seam allowance, removing the pins in the process.

4 Secure the top of the seam on the sewing line and slide a length of boning into the sleeve created by the satin bias and seam. Cut the boning to the correct length.

Finishing edges

Methods of seaming that do not enclose the raw edges require further finishing. Here are a number of suggestions to choose from. These techniques are also useful for hems where the cut edge is visible and for finishing the edges of facings.

Overcasting/zigzag

Modern sewing machines offer a variety of stitches, including some for finishing edges. Choose one of these or an ordinary zigzag to finish raw edges.

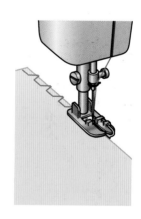

1 Fit an overcasting foot to the sewing machine and set to zigzag or choose a preset overcasting stitch, if available.

2 Sew over the edge of the fabric with the metal finger of the presser foot placed directly over the cut edge.

Zigzag

Sewing right on the fabric edge without an overcasting presser foot causes the edge to pull in and crumple up into a ridge. This alternative takes longer but gives a flat finish.

1 If an overcast foot is not available, sew a line of zigzag stitching ¼ in (6 mm) inside the fabric edge.

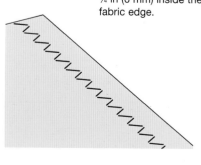

2 Trim away the excess fabric beyond the stitching.

Serger

Using a serger to finish raw edges is a fast method and gives a manufactured appearance. Use three threads for most fabrics and four on heavier coating fabric.

1 Set the serger for balanced three-thread stitching.

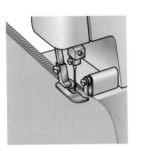

2 Skim the raw edge of the fabric with the serger, removing a minimal amount with the blade. This gives a manufactured appearance to the edge.

Binding

Bias binding is used to encase and finish a cut edge. It provides a strong, tidy finish and can be decorative, too. The advantage of the bias, or crosswise, grain means the binding follows a shaped edge without producing wrinkles and folds.

1 Press ready-made bias binding in half, making sure the edges meet precisely.

2 Slide the cut edge into the folded binding and pin through all layers to hold them together.

3 Set the sewing machine to straight stitch and sew from the right side close to the binding edge and through all layers below.

Hong Kong finish

This looks similar to a bias-bound edge but is not as bulky, having one less layer. It gives a neat and delicate finish to a raw edge and is both functional and decorative. Like a bias-bound edge, it is smooth and wrinkle-free.

1 Cut a 1¼-in (3-cm) wide strip of fine silk or lining at 45 degrees to the fabric grain.

2 Place one edge of the bias strip to the edge of the fabric with right sides facing. Pin and sew ¼ in (6 mm) from the edge.

3 Trim the seam allowance to ⅛ in (3 mm) then wrap the bias strip over and around the seam allowance to cover it.

4 From the right side, pin and stitch "in the ditch"— where the strip meets the fabric—to hold the strip in place.

5 Trim away any excess seam allowance from the underside to reduce bulk. As the strip is cut on the bias, it will not fray.

Darts

Darts help to create shape in garments by pinching out a wedge of cloth to better follow the contour of the figure. Often used at the waist or bust of skirts, dresses, and tops, they are either single and triangular shaped, or double-ended with points at both ends.

Single dart

Use a single dart at the waist and bust and curve the shape to match the body contour. Gently sew off the edge of the dart at the point for a smooth finish.

1 Mark the position and size of the dart on the fabric with tailor's tacks or a fade-away pen, transferring the markings from the paper pattern.

2 Fold the dart through the center with right sides together and pin, making sure the markings are matched.

3 Sew the dart with a straight stitch from the wide end to the point. Sew the dart with a slight curve to prevent a sharp point at the end.

4 Tie off the thread ends to secure the seam, or reverse stitch into the fabric close to the fold. Press to one side.

Double-ended dart

A double-ended dart is often used where there is no horizontal waist seam to pinch out the fabric to follow the shape of the figure.

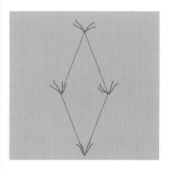

1 Transfer the pattern markings from the paper pattern to the fabric.

2 Fold the dart in half vertically with the right sides facing, matching up the pattern markings. Pin the dart.

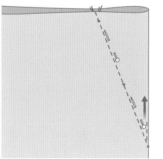

3 Start in the middle of the dart and stitch to one end point. Secure the thread ends.

4 Turn the garment over and sew from the center of the dart to the opposite point. Overlap two or three stitches to lock the seam at the middle of the dart and finish the threads at the pointed end.

Hems

Hems are finished edges used to give a neat border at the base of a skirt or dress, pants, or sleeves. They are generally a single or double fold of fabric held in place with hand or machine stitches. The exception is a faced hem where an additional piece, matching the shape of the hem, is sewn on.

Double-folded, machine-stitched hem

Fold the hem up twice to enclose the raw edge and finish with a straight stitch to give a strong hem, with the stitching visible on the surface. Choose a standard color-matched thread for stitching, or lengthen the stitch and use a topstitch thread for a bolder finish.

1 Fold the raw edge to the wrong side of the fabric to the hem level marked.

2 Fold up again and pin in place, enclosing the raw edge inside. Place the pins on the right side of the fabric, since it will be sewn from this side.

3 Topstitch from the right side, catching the folded edge below, and sew all the way around the circumference of the hem. Use a standard color-matched thread for a delicate edge, or a topstitch thread and an 8 spi (3 mm) stitch for a bolder finish.

Faced hem

When a hem edge is very curved and a standard fold-up hem would result in many tucks and gathers in the hem allowance, a faced hem is a better option. It provides a flat finish, and a deep facing works well on full evening skirts and bridal wear because it adds body and weight to the hem. It is held in place with slip or lock stitches.

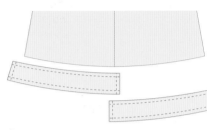

1 Mark the hem length with pins and draw in a hem allowance ⅝ in (1.5 cm) below this. Trim away the excess hem below.

2 Make a pattern of the lower 3 in (7.5 cm) of each skirt panel and cut it out in fabric.

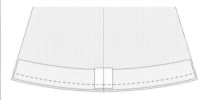

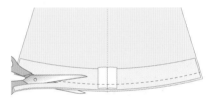

3 Place each facing to its matching panel at the base of the hem with right sides together. Pin on the sewing line, then stitch.

4 Trim the seam allowance to a minimum and press the hem up and into place on the wrong side.

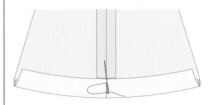

5 Tuck the seam allowances under at the seams and slip stitch together.

6 Turn under the top edge of the facing and hem with a lock or slip stitch.

Hand-finished hem

Fold as described for the double-folded, machine-stitched hem or fold once and neaten the raw edge, but hold the hem in place with regularly spaced hand stitches rather than machining. Hand stitches are hardly visible so the finish is more delicate, although it is not as strong. There are various stitches to choose from and selection depends on the weight and handle of the fabric. Use a small needle when sewing a hem because this encourages smaller stitches, and keep them evenly spaced. Cut shorter lengths of thread, since longer ones tend to knot and tangle.

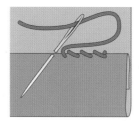

HEMMING STITCH

Use this when a strong finish is required and on medium- and heavier-weight fabrics. On a lighter, finer cloth, hemming stitches would show on the right side.

SLIP STITCH

This stitch is ideal for an almost-invisible hem on most weights of fabric, including light and fine cloth. Slide the needle through the fold of the hem and take a tiny stitch, catching only a few threads of the cloth, on the right side. Keep the stitches well spaced yet even to make them less noticeable.

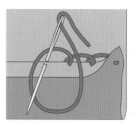

LOCK STITCH

Since each lock stitch is looped around itself, the hem will not come down if the thread breaks. On other hand-sewn hems the entire hem may unravel and become unstitched, but the lock stitches on this hem hold temporarily until a repair can be made. A lock stitch is especially useful on stretch fabric because the stitches move with the fabric.

Rolled hem

For a fine fabric, use a delicate finish like a rolled hem. This is ideal with chiffon or silk for creating floaty sleeves and skirt hems. This can be finished by hand or with a sewing machine or serger.

HAND

1 Run a line of straight stitch ¼ in (6 mm) below the hem line and trim away the excess hem allowance. Press the stitching flat so there are no wrinkles.

2 Roll the edge to the wrong side with your fingers and sew a slip stitch to hold it in place. The line of stitching gives a firm edge to make handling easier.

SEWING MACHINE

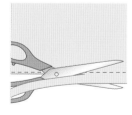

1 Sew a line of straight stitch ¼ in (6 mm) below the hem line and trim away the excess hem allowance. Press the stitching flat so there are no wrinkles.

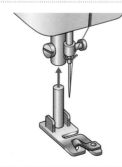

2 Fit a rolled hem foot to the machine and feed the stitched edge into the spiral at the front of the foot. As the fabric is fed into the foot, it will be curled and twisted to form a tiny double hem, enclosing the raw edge inside. Guide the fabric as you sew.

SERGER

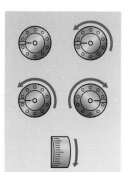

1 Set the serger to rolled hemming according to the manual with matching cones of thread.

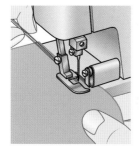

2 Feed the fabric edge under the presser foot at the hem length required. The blade will cut away the excess fabric and the raw edge will be completely covered with stitching.

Zippers

Use zippers for skirts, pants, casual jackets, and dresses. Choose them appropriately and use a suitable method of insertion. Zipper teeth are made from plastic or metal and they can be small and delicate or big and chunky. A concealed zipper has the teeth set at an angle so that when inserted carefully, they appear as part of the seam and are virtually invisible.

Centered zipper

With this method, the teeth are directly below the fold, and the stitching holding it in place on both sides is the same distance away. This is an easy method of sewing in a zipper, so it is ideal for beginners.

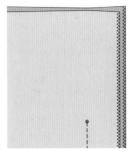

1 Sew a plain seam ⅝ in (1.5 cm) from the edge, leaving a gap where the zipper will be placed.

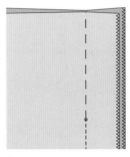

2 Set the sewing machine to the longest straight stitch and continue the seam along the gap for the zipper. This acts as temporary stitching while it is sewn in place.

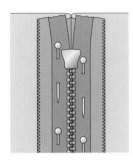

3 Press the seam open, with the wrong side facing up, and place the zipper, face down, over the seam. Make sure it is centered and pin the zipper tape to the fabric on both sides.

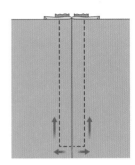

4 Baste the zipper in position, then stitch it in place, sewing from the base to the top on both sides. This prevents twisting and any tucks from gathering at the bottom of the zipper. Finally, remove the temporary stitching.

Lapped zipper

With a lapped insertion, the zipper is offset and placed to one side. Use this method in the center back of skirts and dresses and also for side fastenings.

1 Machine stitch the seam from the base of the zipper to the hem, leaving an opening where the zipper will be placed.

2 Press the seam open, including the part left unstitched.

3 Place the seam over the zipper with the right side facing up. Pin and stitch the right folded edge to the zipper tape, close to the teeth.

4 Close up the zipper and place the left folded edge over the zipper to meet the right folded edge. Pin the left edge through the folded fabric and through the tape below. Stitch from the base of the zipper to the top, removing the pins in the process.

Invisible zipper

An invisible zipper appears like part of the seam with no topstitching visible on the outside. It is a method regularly used in manufacturing, and with the right tools, it is easy to insert these zippers at home. This is useful for velvet and other pile fabrics.

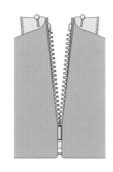

1 Keep the two parts of the seam separate and pin the zipper tape to each side, with right sides facing.

2 Fit a standard zipper foot to the sewing machine and sew each side of the zipper to the fabric edges. These are "holding" stitches to make the next step easier.

3 Open the zipper and fit a concealed zipper foot to the sewing machine. Place the foot over the teeth of the zipper and sew along the length of the teeth. The foot tilts the teeth out of the way as you sew to place the stitches right at the base of the teeth.

4 To finish, with the standard zipper foot fitted to the sewing machine, sew the seam from the base of the zipper to the hem.

Pants zipper

A fly-front completely covers the zipper and is used for pants, shorts, and skirts. For men, the zipper is fitted with the left side over the right. It is the opposite for women. A separate strip or guard is stitched to the inside to complete the fly-front method.

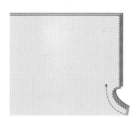

1 Find the position at the base of the zipper where the teeth end. Sew the two front pant pieces together from this point to the inside seam.

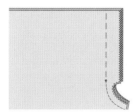

2 With the longest straight stitch, machine baste the opening where the zipper will be placed from the crotch seam to the top of the center front.

3 Finger press the seam open and place wrong side up with the zipper face down over the basted seam. Pin the left side of the tape to the left seam allowance (not through all the layers).

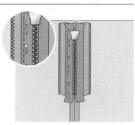

4 Fit the zipper foot to the sewing machine and stitch the tape to the seam allowance, removing the pins in the process. Sew approximately ¼ in (6 mm) from the outside edge of the tape.

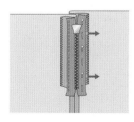

5 Pull the zipper tape to the right and pin in this new position through all layers of fabric.

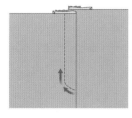

6 Transfer the pins to the right side, making sure the pant front is lying flat with no wrinkles, and baste by hand. Finally, topstitch from the bottom of the zipper to the top edge in a curve, avoiding the teeth of the zipper.

7 Cut a piece of fabric approximately 4 in (10 cm) wide and longer than the zipper. Fold it in half with the right sides together and stitch to make a guard. Trim away the excess seam allowance, turn inside out, and press flat.

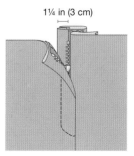

1¼ in (3 cm)

8 Place the guard under the seam allowance on the inside leaving approximately 1¼ in (3 cm) showing under the open zipper. Stitch to the seam allowance.

Fastenings

Fastenings or closures include hooks and eyes, snaps, buttons, and buttonholes. Some are purely functional while others are elaborate and decorative. They come in all sizes and are sewn or clamped in place to secure an opening.

Hooks and eyes/hooks and bars

These are available in all sizes but tiny ones are perfect for holding the top of a zipper in place at the back of a neck. They can also hold a long center-back zipper flat at the curve of the waist. Use the hook with an eye or make your own thread bar.

 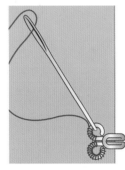

1 Find the best position to hold the opening in a closed position.

2 Work around the wire at the base of the hook and the eye with buttonhole stitch to hold them flat to the fabric.

3 To work a bar opposite the hook rather than an eye, run two or three long stitches with the threads sitting on the surface in the required position.

4 Wrap thread around these long stitches or cover them with blanket stitches. Alternatively, sew a metal bar in place with blanket stitches around the securing wire.

Snaps

Snaps are available in plastic and metal and in a range of sizes. They are typically sewn in position, although some types can be fastened to the fabric with a special pressing tool. The two steps below should be repeated to attach the other half of the snap.

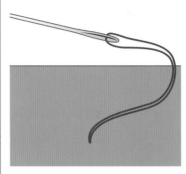 

1 Mark the position on each side of the opening, and using a double thread, secure the end in the fabric.

2 Sew a few threads over each hole, catching the fabric below. The threads should anchor the snap securely.

Buttons

Buttons have two or four holes, or a shank with a hole, so they can be sewn onto fabric. An assortment of sizes and colors is available, and some can be covered with your own choice of fabric for a perfect match to a garment.

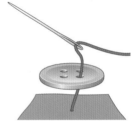 

1 Anchor the thread tail in the fabric in the required position and thread the needle through the first hole.

2 Make several stitches through the eye, catching the fabric below. Do not sew the button tight to the surface, and leave the stitches loose so that a shank can be formed.

 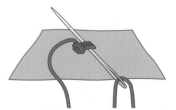

3 With the needle between the button and the fabric, wrap it around the loose central threads several times to form a shank so that the button sits away from the fabric, allowing room for the buttonhole.

4 Take the needle to the wrong side of the fabric and loop through the visible threads a few times to tie them together and to give a neat, secure finish.

Buttons with a shank

Anchor the thread tail in the fabric in the required position. Thread the needle through the hole in the shank and through the fabric several times to hold it in place. Secure the threads.

Buttonholes

Buttonholes were traditionally produced by hand but these days most sewing machines will produce good, functional buttonholes. The alternative to finishing the buttonhole edge with threads is to bind with fabric. The same fabric or a contrasting fabric can be used for this.

AUTOMATIC MACHINE-SEWN BUTTONHOLES

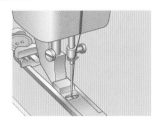

1 Mark the buttonhole position carefully.

2 Select the type of buttonhole required.

3 Place the button in the slider at the rear of the buttonhole foot. This gauges the size of the buttonhole required. Lower the presser foot into position, then sew. A perfectly sized buttonhole will be produced.

4 Open the buttonholes with sharp scissors or a seam ripper through the fabric between the stitches.

MANUAL MACHINE-SEWN BUTTONHOLES

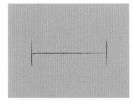

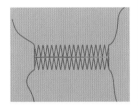

1 Mark the position and length of each buttonhole on the garment.

2 Set the sewing machine to zigzag and shorten the stitch to form a satin stitch. Sew two parallel rows of satin stitches to form the "lips" of the buttonhole.

BOUND BUTTONHOLES

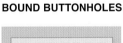

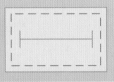

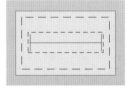

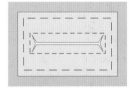

1 Cut a rectangle of fabric on the bias for the bound edges and baste this to the right side of the garment over the buttonhole position.

2 Mark a rectangle for the outer edge of the bound buttonhole and sew over the line. Start in the middle of an edge rather than a corner, and sew twice for extra strength.

3 Cut through the center of the rectangle and close into the corners without snipping any stitches.

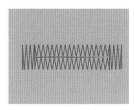

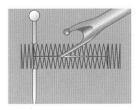

3 Set the zigzag to the same length, but twice the width, and sew the bars or ends of the buttonhole. Tie off the thread ends securely.

4 Open the buttonhole as above. Place a pin at the end to prevent cutting the thread bars at the end.

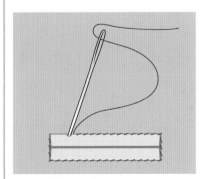

4 Pull the fabric through the slit cut in the buttonhole to the wrong side and tug at the edges until the front lies neatly with two parallel bound edges. Prick stitch around the bound edge.

Sleeves

The shoulders and sleeve head or cap are a prominent part of any garment, so it is essential that they are symmetrical and finished neatly with the easing or gathering at the top of the shoulder.

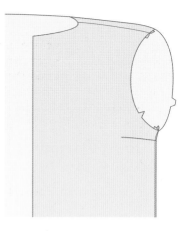

1 Complete the shoulder and side seams of the bodice and the sleeve seams.

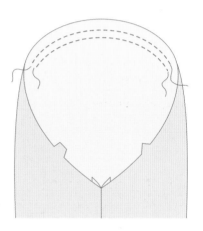

2 Set the sewing machine to the longest straight stitch and sew two parallel rows of stitching across the head of the sleeve. These rows should run from the mid-front to the mid-back of the sleeve and be placed on either side of the seam line.

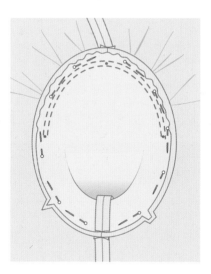

3 Gather the fabric along the stitches and place the sleeve head into the armhole with right sides together and the fabric spread evenly. Most of the fullness will be at the top and slightly to the back. Pin in place on the sleeve side.

4 Return the stitch length to the standard setting—10 spi (2.5 mm)—and sew the sleeve in place along the seam line. Remove the pins in the process.

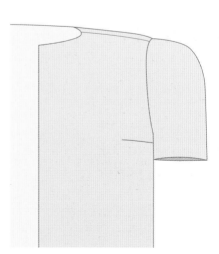

5 Turn right side out and check that a smooth finish has been achieved without any tucks in the seam.

Collars

A shirt collar is made up of a "stand" that sits upright and close to the neck, and a "fall" that drops down and lies over the stand. It can be made in one or two pieces and is sewn to the neckline, concealing all the raw edges. An interfacing is used to add rigidity to the collar. A man's dress shirt is stiff while a more casual shirt or blouse will be softer, so the choice of interfacing will vary.

Making a collar

A quick way of making a stiff collar is explained below.

1 Cut out the collar pieces in fabric (two layers), stiff interfacing (one layer), and fine fusible interfacing (one layer). Cut away the seam allowance from the stiff interfacing.

2 Place the trimmed, stiff interfacing to the wrong side of the upper collar in the center and place the lighter interfacing over it with the fusible side down. With an iron, press the layers together to sandwich the stiff interfacing between the lighter interfacing and fabric.

3 Pin and sew the upper and lower collars together with right sides together. Trim, turn inside out, then press lightly. Finish with edge stitching and topstitching if required.

4 Trim away the seam allowance from the stiff interfacing of the collar stand and fuse it to the wrong side of the fabric piece.

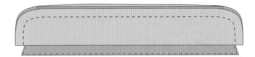

5 Sandwich the prepared collar between the collar stand pieces, matching relevant notches and balance points. Stitch on the seam line, and secure the collar in the process. Trim and snip the seam allowance and turn right side out.

6 Place the outside of the collar stand to the neckline with right sides together, making sure the upper collar will be showing when completed. Pin and sew along the neckline, then trim the seam allowances.

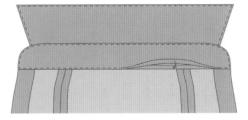

7 Tuck the seam allowance on the remaining edge to the inside and pin to the neckline, hiding the raw edges inside. Edge stitch through the fold and all layers below.

Cuffs

A cuff attached using this manufacturing technique is presewn and ready to be slipped onto the sleeve and topstitched in place. No hand stitching is required and a strong, neat machine finish is achieved.

Attaching cuffs

For a stiff cuff, use a firm interfacing applied with a lighter fusible interfacing to hold it in place. For a softer finish, choose a lighter sew-in or fusible interfacing.

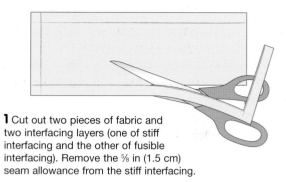

1 Cut out two pieces of fabric and two interfacing layers (one of stiff interfacing and the other of fusible interfacing). Remove the ⅝ in (1.5 cm) seam allowance from the stiff interfacing.

2 Place the stiff interfacing to the wrong side of the cuff in the center and the fusible interfacing over it with the fusible side down. Fuse the layers together with the heat of an iron.

3 Press the seam allowance of the top of the cuff to the wrong side, folding it over the stiff edge of the interfacing. Topstitch ⅜ in (1 cm) from the fold.

4 Place the front and back cuff pieces together with right sides together and raw edges level. Pin and sew on the seam line to join the pieces, leaving the folded side open.

5 Trim and layer the seam allowances, turn right side out, and press the cuff flat. The firm interfacing provides a smooth finish.

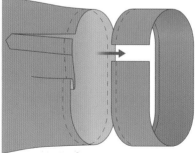

6 Fold the remaining seam allowance into the cuff and press the folded edge. Slip the prepared sleeve into the cuff and pin. Edge stitch from the right side to secure the cuff to the sleeve.

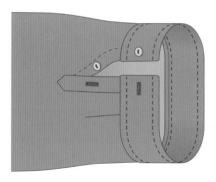

7 Add buttons and buttonholes to complete the cuff.

Tucks and pleats

Tucks and pleats remove fullness in a controlled way and are simply folds of fabric stitched where required. Tucks are often used decoratively and are grouped and evenly spaced. Sometimes tiny tucks are used to give texture to the surface of cloth and are used in a yoke or at a cuff. Larger tucks are folds of fabric at the front of pants or at the head of a sleeve. Pleats are generally large tucks that are pressed or stitched in formation.

Making tucks

Tucks are used to remove fullness and are particularly useful at the waist of pants.

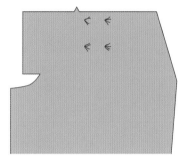

1 Transfer the tuck positions from the paper pattern onto the fabric with a temporary pen or tailor's tacks. Note any arrows used to show the direction of the folds for the tucks.

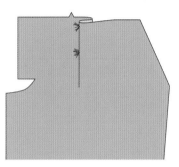

2 Match up the markings and form the tucks, then pin them in place.

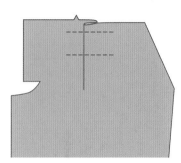

3 Machine baste to hold the tucks in place until they are permanently stitched.

Pin tucks

Pin tucks are made by sewing on the edge of a fold to give texture and interest to an area of a garment. Since only a small amount of fabric is used in a pin tuck, several of these are normally sewn together.

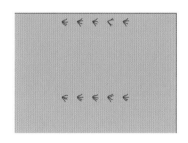

1 Mark the position and length of each tuck carefully with a temporary pen, chalk, or tailor's tacks.

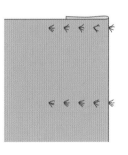

2 Fold the fabric along the first marks with the wrong sides together.

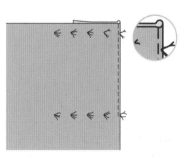

3 Set the sewing machine to straight stitch and sew along the fold. Take the thread tails through the eye of a needle and finish the ends on the wrong side.

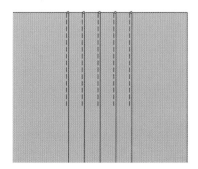

4 Prepare the remaining pin tucks to produce them over the surface of the fabric.

Inverted pleat

An inverted pleat appears as two facing folds and is often seen in skirts, jacket linings, or shirt pockets. An inverted pleat will be stitched for part of its length and the remaining length will hang free.

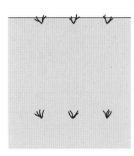

1 Mark the position of the pleat, transferring the balance points from the paper pattern with tailor's tacks.

2 Fold the fabric with right sides together, matching the tailor's tacks accurately, and pin. Sew the required length and finish with reverse stitching.

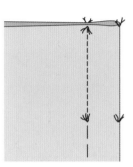

3 Set the sewing machine to the longest straight stitch and baste the remaining length of the seam below the pleat. These are temporary stitches and need not be secured at each end.

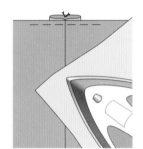

4 Press the entire length of the pleat so that the center lies directly below the seam. Remove the temporary stitches.

Box pleat

A box pleat is often seen at the center back of a shirt and is held in place by the yoke seam. This provides extra fabric to allow for ease of movement.

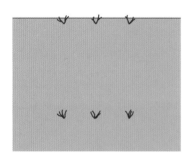

1 Transfer the markings from the paper pattern to the fabric.

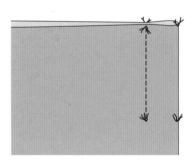

2 Fold the fabric with wrong sides together, matching up the markings accurately. Pin and sew the required length and finish the seam with reverse stitching.

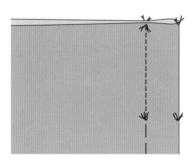

3 Set the sewing machine to the longest straight stitch and sew the remaining length of the seam below the pleat. These are temporary stitches and need not be secured at each end.

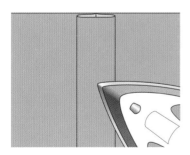

4 Open up the pleat and center it over the seam. Press the entire length of the pleat to sharpen the folds, then remove the temporary stitches.

Elastic

Elastic can be inserted into a casing or sewn directly to the edge of fabric. The former is the traditional method, but direct sewing is used in manufacturing and can be copied at home.

Sewing a casing for elastic

The elastic is fed through a tunnel formed by a topstitched, double-folded edge.

1 Sew up the seams of the garment to form a continuous circumference.

2 Press the edge of the fabric under by ¼ in (6 mm) to the wrong side. Press again, folding the edge to the wrong side, to a width of the elastic plus ⅛ in (3 mm). Pin in place.

3 Set the sewing machine to straight stitch and sew the folded edge to the fabric to form a casing. Sew over the first three stitches with the last three to secure the stitching. Edge stitch the outer folded edge. This will keep casing flat.

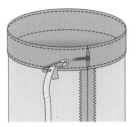

4 Unpick a few stitches in the seam of the casing. With a safety pin attached to the end of the elastic, feed it through the casing. Secure the ends of the elastic and cut off the excess.

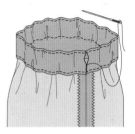

5 Slip stitch the opening in the seam to close the casing.

Sewing elastic and quarter pinning

Sewing elastic directly to the edge gives a neat, modern finish. The trick to attaching the elastic evenly along the length is to divide the fabric and elastic into sections to make it easier to deal with the stretch uniformly. Use this method to attach elastic to a slip or a lightweight skirt.

1 Cut the elastic to length. As a rough guide, this is four-fifths of the measurement to allow for stretch as it is sewn. Form the elastic into a circle and sew the ends together.

2 Divide and mark the elastic into four equal parts, and do the same with the edge where the elastic is to be attached.

3 Match the quarter points and pin them together to hold the sections.

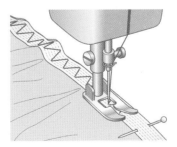

4 Set the sewing machine to a three-step zigzag stitch. Place the elastic to the edge of the fabric on the wrong side and sew a few stitches to anchor the start. Gently pull the elastic until it lies flat over the fabric and stitch the layers together. Continue around the circumference of the fabric.

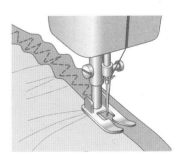

5 Next, fold the edge to the wrong side of the cloth and stitch again with a three-step zigzag to enclose the elastic and hold it in position. Pull gently to sew as before.

Interfacing, underlining, and lining

These are layers added to the inside of a garment to alter and improve the outside. Interfacings are used in specific areas like collars, cuffs, and facings to give support, while underlinings are used for an entire panel of a garment and are cut out and attached to the wrong side before being sewn. Underlinings alter the weight and improve the handle or drape of a cloth.

Interfacing

Interfacings can be sewn in, but these days many are fused in place with the heat of an iron.

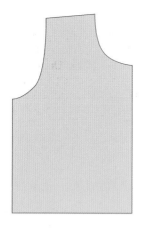

1 Cut the fabric pieces of the garment and place face down on the ironing board.

2 Cut out the interfacing and place it over the wrong side of the fabric in the correct position with the fusible side down. Trim away any interfacing that extends beyond the fabric edge so it does not adhere to the ironing board cover.

3 Hover the iron just above the interfacing and fabric and press the steam button to warm and moisten the materials, but do not place any pressure on them. This shrinks both layers.

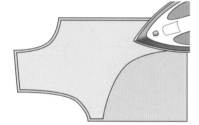

4 Reposition the interfacing over the fabric and apply light pressure and steam to fuse the two layers together. This prevents any bubbles or wrinkles from forming.

Linings

A lining covers the inside of a garment, hiding the seams and raw edges beneath it. It nicely finishes off a jacket, skirt, or dress so that it slides over the body when putting it on and does away with the need for a slip or underskirt.

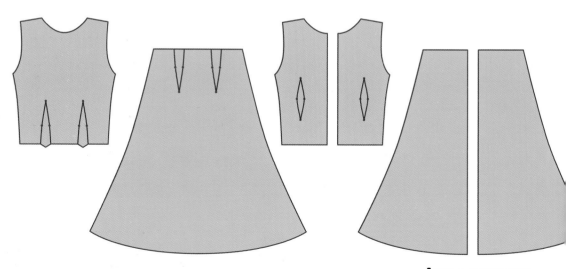

1 Unless lining pattern pieces are included in a paper pattern, cut out the same panels as the dress fabric.

Underlining

An underlining covers an entire panel; they are most common in couture garments to change the handle or characteristics of a fabric. Underlining is often used to prevent a straight skirt from wrinkling or to give more body to a lightweight silk evening skirt. It is used in addition to a lining, not instead of it.

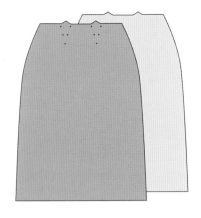

1 Choose a suitable underlining; silk organza, cotton lawn, or lining are often used as an added layer depending on whether a crisp, soft, or heavy finish is needed. Cut it out using the paper pattern pieces.

2 Place the underlining to the wrong side of the dress fabric and pin through the center.

3 With the right side facing up, baste the edges together. For large, gathered skirt pieces, use a sewing machine to baste the layers together. For a straight skirt, shape the pieces so the dress fabric is fractionally larger than the underlining layer, since it has farther to travel around the body.

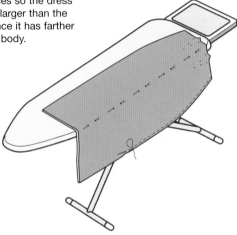

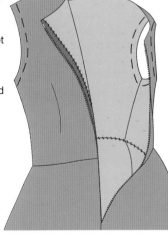

4 Treat the joined layers as one and continue to construct the garment. Finish with a lining to conceal the seams and layers inside.

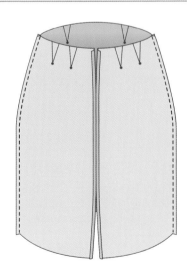

2 Construct the lining in the same way as the dress or skirt, pressing the seams open and folding tucks in the position of darts. Leave an opening where the zipper will be inserted.

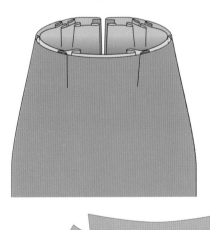

3 Attach the lining to the garment. In the case of a skirt this is normally at the waist, and for a jacket it will be around the interior of the facings. A two-piece dress will be joined at the waist and the bodice pieces will be hand sewn to the waist.

Glossary

Apex
Bust point.

Armscye
This is the armhole measurement.

Balance points
Dots and marks printed on the pattern to match and join when constructing a garment.

Basic block pattern
This is a basic pattern produced from standard measurements before any style has been incorporated. Designs are made from these basic blocks.

Bias/cross grain of fabric
The diagonal direction of fabric between the warp and the weft threads.

CB
Abbreviation used for center back.

CF
Abbreviation used for center front.

Cutting layout
The manufacturer's guide to laying pattern pieces on fabric in the most economical way and keeping pieces "on grain" or on fold lines, and so on. A number of layouts are provided for different fabric widths and pattern sizes.

Dart
A dart is a wedge of fabric that is pinched out of a garment to allow shaping or to remove excess fabric.

Dress form
A mannequin used to assist in the sewing of garments.

Ease
Ease refers to the amount of space built into a sewing pattern—in addition to body measurements—to allow movement and to achieve the required garment silhouette.

Finger pressing
Some fabrics (for example those with natural fibers) respond to handling better than others (for example those from synthetic fibers) and some small areas or seams are better pressed into place using your finger, as an iron would flatten a whole area or create too sharp a finish.

Fold line
Used to describe the position of pattern pieces to be placed on folded fabric. The fabric is folded, right sides together, usually lengthwise so that the selvages are together. A directional arrow on the pattern tissue indicates how to place the piece on the folded fabric.

Grain line
The fabric grain is the direction of the woven fibers. Straight or lengthwise grain runs along the warp thread, parallel to the selvages. Crosswise grain runs along the weft, perpendicular to straight grain. Most dressmaking pattern pieces are cut on the lengthwise grain, which has minimal stretch.

High hip
The high hip is approximately 2 in–4 in (5 cm–10 cm) below the waist and just above the hip bones.

Hip
The hip is the fullest part of the figure and is approximately 7 in–9 in (17.5 cm–23 cm) below the waist.

Underlining
This is a separate layer of fabric cut the same as the panels of dress fabric and placed to the wrong side. The panels are placed together then sewn up as one. Using an interlining or underlining changes the characteristics of the original fabric either to make it heavier, crisper, or less transparent.

Sleeve head
Sometimes referred to as a sleeve cap—the upper part of the sleeve that fits into the shoulder. Not to be confused with a cap sleeve, which is a small sleeve covering the very top of the shoulder.

Sloper
This is a template from which patterns are made and also known as a basic pattern block.

Slub
An uneven thread woven into fabric resulting in an interesting textured surface.

Spi
"Stitches per inch" is used to indicate the stitch length. This measurement is often shown in millimeters.

Stitch in the ditch
Also called "sink stitch," this is where pieces are held together by stitching through an existing seam. Used on waist bands and on Hong Kong finishes.

Truing a line
This is where a line on a pattern is slightly altered to make it smooth and adjust the fit. Often used when transferring adjustments from a toile to a pattern.

Underwrap
The extension on a waistband for the fastening.

Index

Credits

Quarto would like to thank the following agencies and manufacturers for supplying images for inclusion in this book:

Getty Images p.2, 154–155
Photoshot p.16–17, 48–49, 134
Rex p.135

Baby Lock, www.babylock.com, p.10cr
Burda, www.burdastyle.com, p.23b, 25b, 27b, 29b, 30b, 32br
Butterick, http://butterick.mccall.com, p.29b
Janome, www.janome.co.uk, p.10cl
McCall, www.mccall.com, p.21b, 27b
Philips, www.philips.co.uk, p.10b
Simplicity, www.simplicity.com, p.21cl, 23cr, 27b, 32bl

All step-by-step and other images are the copyright of Quarto Publishing plc. While every effort has been made to credit contributors, Quarto would like to apologize should there have been any omissions or errors—and would be pleased to make the appropriate correction for future editions of the book.

Author's ackowledgments

I would like to thank my husband for his support and encouragement during the process of writing this book. Thank you to Burda for very kindly providing paper patterns and to Martin Norris for photography. Thanks also to all involved at Quarto, especially Jackie Palmer for design and finally Chelsea Edwards for her day-to-day help and coordination of the project.